HEART HEALTHY HOSPITALITY

Low Fat Breakfast Recipes From

THE MANOR AT TAYLOR'S STORE

Bed and Breakfast Country Inn

Mary Lynn Tucker

Kia Ora Publications
Rt. 1, Box 533
Wirtz, VA 24184

1 (800) 248-6267

Cover photographs by: Lee Tucker

Library of Congress Card Catalog Number 94-96897
ISBN 0-9644780-0-5

DEDICATED TO

DR PATILLO ELIZABETH DONALD,

WHOSE LIFE WORK WAS DEVOTED TO

NUTRITION EDUCATION AND RESEARCH.

WITH A LITTLE HELP FROM MY FRIENDS...

Nothing of value is ever accomplished alone. All of life's education, experiences, and relationships are incorporated in our efforts. If we are fortunate, those efforts coalesce into a creation that adds to the education and experience of others ... and the cycle goes on. Writing this cookbook has been that type of effort for me, and it is my hope that it will add something new to your life.

The list of individuals who have influenced the production of this cookbook would be nearly as long as the text itself. The project has taken several years and evolved through several stages. My attempt to recount that process and give credit where credit is due is certain to fall short and overlook a very important contributor. Nonetheless, I would like to acknowledge the most obvious of assistance I received in creating this book to share with you.

First and foremost is my partner in the B&B, and in life, Lee. If it weren't for his patience, encouragement, vision, and love, absolutely none of this would have ever transpired. He has functioned as recipe inventor, editor, cover designer, and chief of inspiration ... and deserves as much credit as I for this book.

The wonderful staff at The Manor at Taylor's Store is equally responsible for the successful completion of this project. Agatha Dudley, Debbie Leatherman, Nancy Crow, Denny Laughlin, Barbara Bell, and Martha Garst ... our B&B "family" ... each share their special talents with our guests, and each contributed additional feedback, assistance, and encouragement throughout the conception and execution of this project. It truly could not have happened without their help!

Moving a dream into reality often requires the input of someone who is not "family" ... someone who believes in your idea, has the expertise, and is willing to nurture and encourage as though he was "family". Such a special friend I found in Tracy Winters, our publisher. His assistance was essential ... from the inception of the idea ... through the trials and tribulations of writing and editing ... to the final finished product.

For their loving support and friendship, which makes everything I do easier, I am most grateful to Becca Klingel, Carol Scott, Neva Hart, Carol Beville, and Sara Shields.

I suppose the ultimate debt of gratitude goes to our guests. Without their repeated requests for recipes and their ongoing inquiries about the progress of the cookbook over the last few years, I might not have been prodded along through the journey of this production. Their enjoyment of our B&B, evidenced by their frequent return visits, has been a marvelous source of satisfaction and a stimulus for us to continue to offer them the best we can. True friends do bring out the best you have to offer, so my tremendous thanks to all for helping to make this effort my best!

TABLE OF CONTENTS

WELCOME TO THE MANOR AT TAYLOR'S STORE BED AND BREAKFAST!

Entering the estate between the massive brick columns introducing "Taylor's Store Circa 1799", you immediately get the feeling that you have entered another world. The driveway winds past the Chardonnay vineyard, the original 18th century granary from Taylor's Store, and ancient oaks to the circular drive in front of The Manor. The door between the stately white columns opens to reveal an elegantly restored and furnished plantation home. You are immediately treated to warm Southern hospitality and made to feel at home. You know you are going to experience one of Virginia's finest B&B inns!

Lee and I found the Manor one sunny Sunday afternoon, while on one of our regular weekend drives to search for the perfect home to create a B&B. We had realized shortly after we were married in 1984 that running a B&B was something we both wanted to do. It seemed that every aspect of innkeeping fit us perfectly. We had successfully renovated a home together (even wallpapering... which friends had warned us not to attempt in the first year of marriage!) and really enjoyed that process. We both loved to cook and had developed quite a repertoire of delicious, healthful meals. We looked forward to meeting and visiting with guests from all over the world. We both wanted to live on a farm ... Lee wanted to plant a vineyard and make wine ... I wanted horses and big dogs. We had travelled extensively and stayed at B&Bs, taking notes on things we liked and wanted to do in our own. We were ready to get started!

Our "B&B search" took us throughout the countryside all the way around Roanoke ... we knew we'd know it when we saw it. And we did! Within minutes of walking in, we knew that we'd found our "B&B Home". The house had undergone some renovation in the early 70's, but the project was left uncompleted due to the death of the owner. Therefore, we didn't have to start from scratch, ripping out walls and such, but we did have a considerable amount of work to do before welcoming our first guest.

We moved in in October, 1986 and our first guest arrived in December of that year (no matter that she walked over boards to get in the front door and slept in an unpainted, undecorated room). The renovation project required four years of intensive work to complete the 6 guestrooms and common areas (though, in many ways, we never see it as being "completed" ... rather, ongoing). The grounds of the estate are likewise an ongoing project, from the maintenance of ponds, lawns, and pastures to the recent creation of the Colonial period garden.

The development and maintenance of The Manor and surrounding estate is truly a labor of love for both Lee and me. The physical environment is only one aspect of this project. Perhaps the most rewarding aspect of B&B innkeeping is the opportunity to meet, become friends with, and serve our wonderful guests. After eight years in business, so many of our guests are old friends that have come back to visit again and again. We thoroughly enjoy finding new ways to show them how special they are to us!

One of the ever-changing and ever-improving expressions of our hospitality is the breakfast we offer our guests. From the very beginning, our goal was to offer "heart-healthy" gourmet menus. In 1986, before the "low fat revolution", this was quite a surprise to guests ... some whom expected the traditional Southern breakfast of bacon, eggs, grits, biscuits, gravy, and extra butter. Neither of us could, in clear conscience, feed people we cared so much about like that. Lee, in his work as a physician and pathologist, had seen first hand the ravages of heart disease ... and had been a devotee of preventive dietary practices for years. I was a Family Nurse Practitioner with a Master's degree in Public Health. My professional background was in nutrition and lifestyle education of patients with chronic diseases, such as diabetes and heart disease. It seemed a natural forum for our ongoing mission of public education about preventive health practices ... subtle, yet effective ... to serve guests a delicious meal which is (surprise!) also low-fat. Now, in 1994, most of our guests are already conscious of the benefits of low-fat eating ... and appreciative of our bounteous and healthful breakfasts.

By design, our inn also provides the other elements of a healthful lifestyle. Opportunities for exercise abound, including hiking, swimming, canoeing, and working out in the exercise room. The very setting is conducive to stress management ... wide, open rural space and beautiful pastoral and waterfront vistas. To sit in the gazebo by the spring-fed ponds at sunset and listen to the night sounds is meditative. A soak in the hot tub accompanied by relaxing music and a moonlit night provides instant stress relief. For many of our guests, just getting away from the hustle-bustle of city life and their daily routine to spend a few days with their special person is enough to rejuvenate and re-energize them.

We are now extending our mission of caring for our guests, by offering our recipes and tips for low-fat cooking, that they might further integrate healthful eating into their lives at home.

This cookbook is the outgrowth of over eight years of hosting and repeated requests for recipes. Bookstores are now carrying many low-fat cookbooks, but most are short on breakfast recipes. Since breakfast is the one meal in which people seem to have the hardest time creatively cutting the fat, we hope that this cookbook will fill that need. We also hope that it will help our cherished guests and friends along their journey towards their own optimum wellness, enjoying every bite along the way.

HEART HEALTHY
COOKING

WHAT IS HEART-HEALTHY COOKING?

In my previous life, before innkeeping, I was a registered nurse and a family nurse practitioner. I worked with patients with a variety of chronic diseases - diabetes, heart disease, obesity - to help them and their families to learn more about their health problems. We worked together, helping them make changes in their diets and lifestyles to better manage their health problems. In that position, I learned a lot about nutrition and its effects on health. I also learned a lot about the process of change in human habits. In each educational relationship with a patient, I found two levels of learning necessary to successful lifestyle change. First was basic education about the disease and the recommended treatment - medication, diet, exercise. Second, was counselling them through the process of change necessary to make major lifestyle changes. This second level of teaching and counselling was perhaps the most critical to the patient's successful management of his disease. Knowing what to do is one thing ... being motivated to follow through with what you know to do is quite another!

My patients taught me again and again that setting up unrealistic goals for change, or trying to change too much too fast just resulted in frustration ... for everyone. The most successful cases I remember were individuals who set moderate goals and were pleased with gradual progress in reaching them. It makes sense that a similar approach would work best for those of us who wish to make changes in diet/exercise/lifestyle to prevent health problems.

The first few chapters of this book will help you with the first step of understanding "heart healthy cooking". I have included a brief review of current nutrition recommendations for healthy people in this chapter. The subsequent chapters include a simple explanation of how to read labels to decipher what is in the foods you buy, followed by suggestions for modifying your own recipes to lower fat and increase fiber. With this basic information, you will have the tools to make healthful nutrition decisions.

Step two, or the gradual learning to select and like foods that are lower in fat and higher in fiber, will be an ongoing process for you and your family. It is my hope that some of the delicious recipes offered in this book will encourage you in that process.

Considering that food and nutrition have been essential to man's survival since the beginning of time, it is surprising that the major research comprising the science of nutrition has been a fairly recent phenomenon. In many ways, what the body needs for nourishment and growth, how it uses nutrients, and how appetite and food intake are regulated are still poorly understood. This is in part because conducting controlled scientific experiments in this field is difficult to impossible. Research is able to correlate particular foods and nutritional patterns with particular outcomes, but unable to determine a direct cause and effect to these scenarios. There are too many other variables integral in the way people live their lives that also have an effect on health outcomes. For example, studies that correlate a low cancer rate with diets found in some third world countries cannot remove the obvious influence of other factors in these environments. Tribal cultures in the outback of Australia may not eat much fat, but they also don't drive cars, watch T.V., smoke cigarettes, etc., etc.... so what factor, or combination of factors actually cause cancer?! With the obvious exception of blatant nutritional deficiencies and their resulting pathologies, most of what we presume to know about nutrition comes from studies which observe large samples of individuals and correlate variables in their lives, including dietary patterns, with health outcomes. Such a study was sponsored less than twenty years ago by the U.S. government. In 1977, the Senate Select Committee on Nutrition and Human Needs published its study analyzing the "typical American diet". The goal of the resulting new nutritional guidelines was to prevent many of the nation's major killers - heart disease, cancers of colon and breast, stroke, high blood pressure, obesity, diabetes, arteriosclerosis, and cirrhosis of the liver, all of which have been linked to the American diet. By 1980, the USDA and HEW had published a report on preventive medicine and a pamphlet entitled, "Nutrition and Your Health: Dietary Guidelines for Americans". This new approach to nutrition has subsequently re-shaped the dietary habits of our society and the food industry in this country.

The general guidelines recommended for healthy Americans include:

* Eat a variety of foods
* Maintain ideal weight
* Avoid a lot of fat, saturated fat, and cholesterol
* Avoid a lot of sodium and salt
* Avoid a lot of sugar
* Eat foods with starch and fiber
* Drink only moderate amounts of alcohol

The basic tenets of this approach to health are variety and moderation. Gradual, permanent change towards healthful dietary choices is preferable to a fanatical campaign to eradicate all fat, sugar, and salt (which could result in unpalatable food and a quick reversion to old eating habits).

Since heart disease prevention has been a major target of the modern dietary recommendations, the American Heart Association has developed its own guidelines which are considered safe and prudent for all healthy American adults. In addition to the above guidelines, the AHA suggests:

* Total fat intake should be less than 30% daily calories
* Cholesterol intake should not exceed 300 mg/day
* Carbohydrate should make up 50% or more of calories, with emphasis on complex carbohydrates
* Sodium intake should not exceed 3 g/day

Dietary intake is only one of the controllable risk factors associated with the development of coronary heart disease. Other risk factors include blood cholesterol levels, high blood pressure, smoking, and physical inactivity. All of these risk factors are within personal control, whether through diet, exercise, lifestyle, or medication.

Our "heart-healthy" recipes have been developed and selected with the basic principles of low-fat, low cholesterol, and high-fiber intake in mind ... as well as the philosophy of moderation in all things. Some of the recipes included are "special occasion" foods ... not low enough in fat for daily consumption, but not high enough to exceed recommended guidelines. All the recipes are modified to provide lower fat than the traditional recipes for the same foods.

The following sections will help you select foods at the market that are compatible with the guidelines for health and help you modify your own recipes to lower fat/raise fiber. Remember that the goal is gradual, palatable change ... learning to enjoy more healthful foods.

Nutrition Facts

Serving Size 1 Bar (42g)
Servings Per Container 24

Calories 140
Calories from Fat 0

Amount/Serving	%DV*	Amount/Serving	%DV*
Total Fat 0g	0%	**Total Carbohydrate** 35g	12%
Saturated Fat 0g	0%	Dietary Fiber 3g	12%
Cholesterol 0mg	0%	Sugars 14g	
Sodium 5mg	0%	**Protein** 2g	

Vitamin A 10% (100% as Beta Carotene)   •   Vitamin C 0%
Calcium 0%   •   Iron 6%

*Percent Daily Values are based on a 2,000 calorie diet. Your daily values may be higher or lower depending on your calorie needs:

	Calories	2,000	2,500
Total Fat	Less than	65g	80g
Sat Fat	Less than	20g	25g
Cholesterol	Less than	300mg	300mg
Sodium	Less than	2,400mg	2,400mg
Total Carbohydrate		300g	375g
Dietary Fiber		25g	30g

Calories Per Gram:
Fat 9 • Carbohydrate 4 • Protein 4

LABEL LOGIC
MAKING "HEART HEALTHY" SELECTIONS AT THE MARKET

In May, 1994 selecting healthful foods from the grocery shelves became much easier. The new labelling rules enforced by the FDA and USDA are compatible with currently recommended dietary guidelines. Now it's up to us as consumers to learn to interpret the information on the label and be able to translate it into healthy food choices. This primer in "label-ese" should help make that job a bit easier for you.

"Serving size" has thankfully been revised to reflect realistic portions for real people. In the past, this was often deceptively small and portrayed foods in a more favorable light. The public may have concluded that the fat and/or calorie content of what they were eating was much less than it actually was.

"Calories per serving" is not as important in healthful food selection as "calories from fat", which is now included on the label. You have to do a little math to determine the percentage of fat that this represents, in order to stay within the less-than-30% guideline. Simply divide the fat calories by total calories to come up with the percentage of calories from fat.

"Nutritional components" are now easier to read than before, with the nutritional content of the product listed, in grams or milligrams, directly next to the component. Each component is then expressed in terms of the percentage of daily value, or the percentage of a recommended intake that this serving represents, based on a 2000 calorie/day intake. This information is a bit misleading ... and should not be confused with the previously figured percentage of fat in this serving of food. One problem with this information is that many people should consume either more or less than this 2000 calorie/day, so individual adjustment in the "daily value" would have to be made accordingly. Also, most people don't know how many calories they take in as a daily average. The best use of this information is to observe the nutrients you want to avoid in excess (fat, saturated fat, cholesterol) and keep the percentage points of those items low while favoring total carbohydrate and dietary fiber.

The "guidelines for 2,000 calorie diet" is included on the label to assist consumers in assessing and monitoring their total daily intake of listed nutrients. Again, this may be too much or too little for a given individual.

Without keeping complicated records of what you've eaten and plan to eat, the easiest way to use the provided information is to adhere to these basic tenets:

* The lower the fat, the better. Keep your total to less than 30% of daily calories, with saturated fat less than 10% of the total.

* Dietary cholesterol should be less than 250-300 mg/day. This is most easily accomplished by limiting dairy and animal products.

* With salt (sodium chloride), anything above 2,400 mg is too much. Total intake below 2,000 is ideal since excess salt may contribute to high blood pressure in some individuals.

* The higher the fiber, the better. 25-30 grams/day is suggested and it is difficult to get this much dietary fiber without a very concerted effort.

* The majority of your diet should be carbohydrates, 55-60% of calories, or more. Breads, cereals, fruits, and vegetables are the best sources for complex carbohydrates. The less processed, cooked, or refined a food is, the higher in complex carbohydrates.

Additional nutrition education is provided on the food label in the form of conversion factors for grams to calories. It is interesting to note that both protein and carbohydrate have 4 calories/gram, while fat is a whopping 9 calories/gram. Not a bit of wonder that high fat foods, being more calorically dense, are associated with an excess total caloric intake resulting in obesity. For your interest, alcohol contains 7 calories/gram (no, wine doesn't count as a fruit and beer isn't considered a grain!).

It should be noted that the labelling requirements are focused primarily on prepared and packaged foods. Therefore, understanding labels will provide you only one part of your growing nutrition awareness. The remainder involves becoming conscious of the fat, cholesterol, and fiber content of unlabeled foods, such as meats, cheeses, nuts, grains, and fresh fruits and vegetables.

The progress in public education that the new labelling system represents is a big step in the direction towards a healthier America. However, there are still some misleading claims permissible on packaged foods. "Low fat", "Low cholesterol", and "High fiber" are relative terms, with no standards for definition. In fact, they are easily manipulated as marketing ploys and should signal a red-flag to the wise consumer. "Organic", "Natural", "Healthy", and "Fresh" are equally unreliable descriptives ... usually used to portray a nutritious image for marketing purposes rather than educate the consumer to make a healthful food choice. Yes, in spite of the progress in labelling, it is still "buyer beware" when you make your decisions in the market ... the more you learn about the nutritional attributes of foods, the better able you will be to make nutrition-wise choices.

MODIFYING YOUR OWN HOUSE SPECIALTIES TO CREATE "HEART HEALTHY" MEALS

We hope that many of the recipes in this cookbook will become family favorites in your home. You will also, no doubt, want to convert some of your old family favorites to create your own "heart healthy" recipes. The first step in doing this is knowing what you are buying at the market, as we discussed in the previous chapter. When you get the groceries home, you can further modify the fat/fiber in your recipes by either changing the cooking technique or substituting the ingredients.

Modifying your own recipes will require some trial and error on your part, but you'll quickly learn what works and what doesn't work with your favorite recipes. You may get some guidance in this process by looking at low fat cookbooks, such as this, and trying the methods or ingredients in recipes similar to yours.

The cooking method you use can easily alter recipes to make them "heart healthier". Some suggested cooking techniques that may be used for low fat cooking include:

* Oven frying - Baking food on a rack in an oven with dry heat. The rack enables all sides to be equally exposed to the heat and yields a crisp coating that imitates deep-fat frying. This is ideal for "frying" fish. French toast may be baked instead of fried, as we do at the inn.

* Braising - This technique is particularly useful for tenderizing lean cuts of meat. First the food is browned using vegetable cooking spray. It is then cooked, tightly covered, in a small amount of liquid at low heat for a long period of time. The long, slow cooking process tenderizes the meat by breaking down the fibers. Refrigerating the braised meat overnight allows the fat that has cooked out in the liquid to congeal on the surface, which can then be removed before serving.

* Broiling and grilling - Both of these techniques allow fat to drip away from the food. Direction of the heat source is the main difference between them.

* Poaching - Foods are cooked in water or other liquid that is held just below the boiling point. This method keeps food moist without adding fat. Poaching in wine or broth can add flavor.

* Sautéing - Food is cooked quickly over direct heat with little fat. Non-stick pans and spraying with vegetable cooking spray can reduce needed fat. Sautéing can also be done in small amounts of broth, wine, or water.

* Steaming - Food is cooked over, not in, boiling water. Nutrients are maintained and flavor may be added by adding herbs or spices to boiling water.

In addition to modifying the cooking technique you use to decrease the fat, you can alter the ingredients in some recipes to make them more heart healthy. Alteration of an ingredient can involve either reducing it, eliminating it, or substituting it. Before altering an ingredient, you will want to determine whether that ingredient, in that amount, is essential to the recipe. This may involve a bit of experimentation to determine. Particularly tricky is the reduction or elimination of fat from baked goods. For all the bad rap they get, fats do play an important role in many recipes, including increasing tenderness and moistness in baked goods and flakiness in pie crusts. In many baked products, the fat (shortening, oil, or margarine/butter) can be reduced by about 1/4 to 1/3 with satisfactory results. Addition of, or substitution with, something to add the moisture you're removing may further improve the recipe. Applesauce, fruit puree, fruit juice, or skim milk are some suggestions. Additional ideas for reducing fat and cholesterol in your own recipes include:

* Use non-fat or low cholesterol dairy products
* Shred or grate cheese to make it go farther, decrease the amount of cheese used by 1/3 to 1/2 and substitute a strong-flavored cheese to achieve a full flavor
* Chilled evaporated skim milk may be whipped into a substitute for whipping cream
* Be careful when substituting reduced-calorie margarine for regular margarine in baked goods - the water that's whipped into reduced-calorie margarine may cause sogginess
* Substitute 2 egg whites, or 1/4 cup egg substitute for each whole egg in a recipe
* Use non-fat mayonnaise or non-fat yogurt in place of mayonnaise
* Non-fat yogurt "cheese" makes a great substitute for sour cream or cream cheese (see recipe on page 154)
* Use skimmed evaporated milk rather than cream
* Make gravy from bouillon, stock, or wine and herbs; thickened with arrowroot powder, flour, or cornstarch. Or try thickening by reduction (cooking to remove water)
* Blenderized low-fat cottage cheese may be substituted for mayonnaise or sour cream
* Refrigerate stocks, soups, stews to condense fat on the surface, then skim off before reheating and serving

Modifying recipes to add fiber is a reasonably simple thing to do. You may try:
* Substitute whole-wheat flour (half the quantity) for all-purpose flour when baking. Whole wheat pastry flour gives a lighter baked product than

regular whole wheat flour. Stone-ground whole wheat flour is the highest in fiber, and results in a denser bread product.

* Add 2 tablespoons unprocessed oat or wheat bran for each cup flour in baking
* Use brown rice, whole wheat, or vegetable-base noodles and pastas
* Serve fresh fruits and vegetables with skin on (scrub well)
* Add sunflower, sesame, poppy seeds for crunch and taste
* Use wheat germ, unprocessed bran, or uncooked oats in salads, casseroles, and muffins or as a light coating for baked chicken or fish
* Add dried fruits to your recipes
* Make your own high-fiber breakfast cereals (see recipes on pages 70, 71, 72, 73)

While reduction of salt is not necessary nor recommended for all healthy people, you may try modifying your recipes by:

* Use fresh or frozen ingredients, rather than canned
* Rather than salt in cooking, use herbs, spices, citrus peel, or fruit juices
* Make your own stock with leftover vegetables rather than using broth bases or bouillon
* You can usually reduce salt in recipes by at least 1/2

While experimenting with your own recipes, keep notes on the cookbook/recipe card, so that you can replicate the changes you've made. Also, magazines such as "Cooking Light" always like to receive recipe modifications from readers. Share your joy of heart healthy cooking with others!

TOUR OF THE MANOR: THE PARLOR

The most striking feature of the parlor (and perhaps of the whole house) is the tall case clock in the parlor. It is truly a special piece. It was designed by Stanford White, the famous architect, in 1903...for a specific home which he also designed. The elaborate carvings on the case replicate the carvings around the front entrance to "Harbor Hill", the Long Island residence of Clarence McKay (whose fortune was made in telegraph around the turn of the century). This magnificent mansion was said to be second only to the Biltmore House in its grandeur, and photographs we have of the home and its furnishings substantiate that claim. When that home was dismantled, the clock found its way to Franklin County and was being stored in a local antique warehouse where Lee and I made its acquaintance.

Lee is a graduate of The University of Virginia, and recognized Stanford White for his work in restoration of the Rotunda there (after a fire in the late 1800's). This historic connection as well as the impressiveness of the clock itself led us to decide that it belonged at The Manor. It is certainly one of the most memorable visual treats for our guests.

The parlor also has some other interesting furnishings. There is a mahogany Victorian aviary, which was made in the Phillipines with elegant carvings and brass fittings. The baby grand piano is a 1936 Wurlitzer, a Christmas gift from Lee to me our first year at The Manor. The loveseat and chairs are late Victorian rosewood pieces which we found at a local estate auction. We have had elderly local women tour the house and say, "You were so lucky to get Minnie Jones' furniture...that is the original upholstery and it is in such good condition because she never let anyone sit on it!". All of these elements create an ambience of elegance in the formal Victorian Parlor.

FIRST COURSE, FABULOUS FRUITS

FOR STARTERS...

Our B&B guests' breakfasts often begin with a cup of our special "Mill Mountain Blend" coffee, which we get from The Mill Mountain Coffee Shop on the Roanoke Farmer's Market. This marvelous place is truly an olfactory wonderland ... with beans of all types being roasted and ground on site. Any hour of the day or evening it is packed with people gathering over a cup of java or pot of tea and enjoying one of their yummy pastries. Our discriminating guests truly appreciate both the regular and de-caf "house blends" that we offer ... or, if they prefer, a cup of tea from our bounteous tea basket.

We serve our breakfast in courses, beginning with a fruit course. This course depends entirely on the time of year and what fresh fruits are available locally. Between seasons, when the fresh fruits aren't up to par, we will creatively use canned fruits or make one of the "Breakfast Drinks" as an appetizer. The "Breakfast Soups" are another original way to start out ... a surprise to most guests, who quickly become converts.

AMBROSIA ... FOOD OF THE GODS (AND GODDESSES)

One of the simplest, yet tastiest, fruit dishes is ambrosia. I recall having had this as a child, served as a dessert with a few cookies on the side. No wonder it seems like a special dish for me to share with B&B guests!

Yes, the coconut does contain those wicked saturated fats ... obviously the ancient Gods who lived on ambrosia didn't worry about atherosclerosis, being endowed with immortality anyway. However, you can still enjoy this tasty dish and relax in the knowledge that the minute amount of coconut oil in each serving is less than 1 teaspoon butter in saturated fat content. For those who wish to avoid saturated fat in any form...the dish is almost as yummy without the coconut. Aphrodite would definitely approve!

4 large, juicy, navel oranges
4 ripe (but still firm) bananas
2 tablespoons orange juice
1/8 cup grated, unsweetened coconut
Optional additions: a sprinkling of
sunflower seeds or toasted almonds

Peel and chop the navel oranges into a bowl. Add the orange juice and coconut and toss well. At this point, you may refrigerate the oranges...and complete the recipe in the morning, just before serving. Peel and slice bananas into bowl with oranges and toss well (but carefully, not to bruise or mash bananas). Serve in attractive bowls ... we use a footed glass dish which has had the edge dipped in a plate of orange juice, then a plate of sugar to create a "sugar halo" around the rim of the dish. Top with a few sunflower seeds or toasted almonds, if desired.

BROILED GRAPEFRUIT A LA CHALET SUZANNE

On the trip to Florida that led Lee and I into innkeeping, one of our most memorable stops was a most magical inn, Chalet Suzanne in Lake Wales. From the eclectic decor, to the serendipitous rainbow leading to the pond outside our window, to the unforgettable gourmet cuisine, this was clearly one of our favorite country inn memories. This grapefruit was served as an appetizer with dinner, and though we don't top ours with the sauteed chicken liver that they did (not exactly a breakfast item) ... I can't fix this dish without reminiscing about Chalet Suzanne.

1 grapefruit, ripe and juicy
1 tablespoon cinnamon-sugar mixture (1 part
    cinnamon to 4 parts sugar)
1 teaspoon melted margarine (I use Promise)
2 strawberries or maraschino cherries

Slice grapefruit in half (we use a scalloping tool to create a wedged edge) and cut around the inner membrane to remove center and seeds. Sprinkle each half with 1/2 teaspoon of melted margarine and 1/2 tablespoon of cinnamon-sugar. Place grapefruit on shallow baking pan and broil just long enough to brown tops and heat to bubbling hot. Top with a fanned strawberry or maraschino cherry.

Serves: two.

TOUR OF THE MANOR: THE DINING ROOM

Lee is truly one of the most versatile and creative people I have ever known! Not only is he skilled at his profession...and talented in music and art...and knowledgeable about everything from sailing to making wines...but he can design, build, and repair anything (a very useful repertoire for an innkeeper!). I love to brag about the fact that he made the beautiful dining room table that our guests have breakfast on. It is crafted of Honduras mahogany and is a replica of a Queen Anne banquet table from Colonial Williamsburg. He actually made the table before we even knew we'd one day have a B&B. Therefore, when we went looking for the right home in which to create our B&B, we had to measure the prospective dining rooms to be sure that the table would fit. Like Cinderella and the glass slipper, when we discovered the Manor, "tried on" the table, and realized it fit...we knew we'd found her!

PEARS WITH STRAWBERRY COULIS

Fresh, poached pears are best with this dish. But canned pears will do if fresh ones aren't available ... and don't need to be poached. You may want to "marinate" the canned pears in a wine/cinnamon/vanilla bean/lemon mixture to add to the interest of the dish if using canned pears. The coulis can be made up ahead of time, frozen in small batches, and thawed the day before you plan to serve.

> 2 cups dry white wine
> 2 1/2 cups water
> 1 cinnamon stick
> 1 vanilla bean
> Zest of 1 lemon
> 4 firm, ripe pears
> 1 cup Strawberry Coulis (recipe below)
> 1/2 cup toasted almond slivers

In a deep saucepan, combine wine, water, cinnamon stick, vanilla bean, and lemon zest. Bring to a boil. Peel pears and gently drop them into poaching liquid, adding water or wine, if necessary, to completely cover the fruit. Cover and simmer 25-30 minutes, or until the pears are tender. Remove from heat. Cool pears in the poaching liquid until ready to serve.

Strawberry Coulis:

> 2 pints fresh or frozen strawberries
> 1/2 teaspoon almond extract
> 1/2 teaspoon vanilla extract
> 2 tablespoons granulated sugar (more to taste,
>   depending on the sweetness of the berries)

Wash and hull fresh berries (or thaw and drain frozen berries). In blender or food processor, puree the berries, adding the extracts and sugar.

TO SERVE: Ladle 1/4 cup strawberry coulis onto serving dish and place 1/2 poached pear on top. Sprinkle with toasted almonds.
Serves: 8 people.

MANOR BANANAS

This low fat version of the famous Bananas Foster is an elegant way to start the day ... without the flambé!

> 1 tablespoon margarine
> 1 lemon, juiced (or 2 tablespoons lemon juice)
> 4 bananas, sliced
> 4 dates, chopped (1/4 cup pre-chopped dates)
> 1 teaspoon cinnamon
> 4 walnut halves, chopped (1/4 cup chopped nuts)
> 1 tablespoon Amaretto or Kahlua
>   (or 1 teaspoon liqueur flavoring)

Melt margarine with lemon juice. Add banana slices, dates, cinnamon, and walnuts. Sauté briefly. Sprinkle with amaretto. Serve in individual plates and garnish with shredded orange zest.
Yield: 4 servings.

GRILLED MELON

If you are grilling out for dinner, you can make these lovely kabobs at the end of your cookout ... and either refrigerate them to serve for breakfast, or serve with coffee for dessert.

> Bamboo skewers (2 for each portion)
> 1 cantaloupe or honeydew melon, cut in thin wedges
>   (a combination of both makes a very
>   pretty presentation)
> 2 kiwi fruit, sliced
> 2 tablespoons melted margarine
> 1 tablespoon lemon juice
> 1 teaspoon chopped fresh mint (1/2 teaspoon dried,
>   if fresh not available)
> Cinnamon and mint sprigs for garnish

Thread several melon wedges and kiwi slices onto each skewer. Run a second bamboo skewer through the fruit to secure the kabob. Melt margarine and stir in lemon juice and chopped mint. Baste fruit with this mixture. Grill 4 inches from medium hot coals until fruits are hot and streaked with brown. Dust with cinnamon and garnish with mint sprigs.
Yield: 6 servings.

GLORIA'S CURRIED FRUIT

My friend and neighbor, Gloria Scott, is one of the most creative cooks I know. She has had a long career in restaurant and catering ... and her love of cooking extends to trying new recipes and sharing them with neighbors. We have been the lucky recipients of her delicious cakes, cookies, and soups on many occasions. This is a recipe from a New Year's Eve Breakfast she made for us!

1 20-ounce can peach halves
1 20-ounce can bing cherries
1 20-ounce can pineapple chunks
1 20-ounce can pear halves
1 11-ounce can mandarin oranges
2/3 cup brown sugar
2 teaspoons curry powder
Juice of one lemon
1/4 cup margarine

Drain fruits well in a colander until all juice has run off, 1-2 hours. Prepare a shallow casserole (8x12-inch or similar size) by spraying with cooking spray. Add fruit. Combine brown sugar and curry powder and mix well. Sprinkle brown sugar mixture over fruits. Sprinkle this combination with lemon juice and dot with margarine. Cover and bake 1 hour in 300° oven.

Yield: About 2 quarts, 12 servings.

SPICY STEWED FRUIT

In the dead of winter, when fresh fruits are nowhere to be found ... this warm mixture of dried fruits is real comfort food.

1 stick cinnamon
1 teaspoon whole clove
1 cup dried, pitted prunes
1 cup dried apricots
1 cup dried apples
1/2 cup raisins
1 cup orange juice
2 cups water
1/4 cup brown sugar

Place cinnamon and cloves in a cheesecloth bag; tie bag, and place in large saucepan. Combine orange juice, water, and brown sugar until brown sugar is dissolved. Add this mixture and fruit to the large saucepan. Bring mixture to a boil. Reduce heat; simmer 30 minutes. Cool slightly; discard the spice bag. Serve warm or cold.

Yield: 6-8 servings.

STRAWBERRY-CHEESE PARFAIT

3/4 cup lowfat cottage cheese
2 teaspoons sugar
1/2 teaspoon almond extract
1/4 teaspoon cinnamon
1 cup sliced fresh strawberries, divided
2 tablespoons granola (see cereal section for recipe)
2 fresh strawberries

Combine first 4 ingredients in blender; process until smooth. To serve, place 1/4 cup strawberries in a tall, champagne flute. Top with 3 tablespoons cheese mixture, 1/4 cup strawberries, 2 tablespoons cheese mixture, and top with 1 tablespoon granola. Repeat procedure with remaining ingredients. Garnish with a fresh strawberry.

Yield: 2 servings.

FRESH FRUIT SALAD DU JOUR

We keep a good supply of whatever fruits are in season on hand and often will combine them into a medley for the breakfast appetizer. All fruits can be mixed with others ... so just be creative and choose for variety of color, texture, and shape.

Then, you may top with a dollop of vanilla yogurt or one of these fruit toppings:

FRUIT CREAM

This rich tasting and healthy cream can be used to top any fresh fruit choice. It is especially delicious dolloped on fresh berries or peaches!

- **2 cups low fat cottage cheese**
- **1 teaspoon honey**
- **1 teaspoon vanilla**
- **2 teaspoons low fat imitation sour cream (or yogurt cheese ... recipe on page 154)**

Mix together first three ingredients in food processor until very smooth. Transfer to small bowl and fold in sour cream. Cover and refrigerate until ready to use. Will keep about 1 week refrigerated.

Makes 2 cups (about 50 cal / 1/4 cup).

APRICOT GLAZE

- **1 (6-ounce) can apricot nectar (3/4 cup)**
- **1 tablespoon honey**
- **1 teaspoon vanilla**

Combine ingredients in blender. Pour over fruit salad and allow the combination to chill together for a few hours.

Yield: 6-8 servings.

APPLE-CHEESE SAUCE

This sauce is especially nice on an apple/grape/banana combination. It can also be used as a crepe filling!

1 cup lowfat cottage cheese
1 cup applesauce
2 tablespoons honey
Cinnamon or nutmeg

Place ingredients in blender and blend until smooth.
Yield: 2 cups or 10-12 servings.

CITRUS-MINT MARINADE FOR MELON

A combination of cantaloupe, honeydew and watermelon balls is enhanced by this marinade. This recipe can only be made in the heat of the summer, when melons are their ripest and the mint that grows profusely around the smokehouse can be harvested.

1 cup orange juice
1/4 cup lime juice
2 tablespoons honey
1 tablespoon chopped fresh mint

Combine ingredients in a saucepan; bring to boil, stirring frequently. Pour into bowl and cover and chill.
When chilled, pour over melon balls and cover and chill for up to 4 hours before serving.
Yield: 6 servings.

NOT-EXACTLY FRIED APPLES

A traditional Southern breakfast is not complete without a side dish of fried apples. We find that this version (while minus the bacon fat that flavors the traditional one) is a lovely accompaniment to many of the dishes that we serve. It is ideal with potato latkes, turkey-sausage gravy with biscuits, or even as a simple side to a ham biscuit.

6 large apples, cored, chopped, but not peeled
1 cup apple cider (or juice)
1 teaspoon cinnamon
1/2 cup brown sugar

Spray large non-stick skillet with cooking spray and heat to medium-high. Add apples and sauté them for one minute, stirring constantly. Add apple cider, cinnamon, and brown sugar. Stir to combine well with apples. Bring to a gentle boil and reduce heat to medium-low. Continue cooking until cider is reduced and juices are thickened. Serve hot.
Yield: 6-8 large servings.

WHERE'S THE STORE?

The name, "Taylor's Store" has led to much confusion and quandary. Often a car will wander into the driveway with a puzzled driver who queries, "Where's the store? I need a loaf of bread".

Taylor's Store was a two-story brick building that stood on the front of the property, just behind where the brick columns are located now. It was opened in 1799 as a general merchandise trading post, serving the local settlers and travellers passing along the old Warwick Road. In 1812, a U.S. Post Office was commissioned to operate in the store, resulting in the entire surrounding community becoming known as "Taylor's Store".

Over the years, Taylor's Store played a central role in the lives of the families of the community. In addition to providing supplies from housewares to farm tools, it served as a gathering place for the daily exchange of news and weekly social activities. Some of the elderly residents of Franklin County still remember the square dances held upstairs at the store.

As the years brought increased mobility to area residents, with automobiles and improved roads, the role of the country store changed. Still supplementing daily needs, both social and material, it no longer filled those primary needs as it had for over a century and a half. Sadly, neglect and time resulted in deterioration of Taylor's Store. It fell into disrepair and was dismantled in the early 1970's.

To commemorate the important role that Taylor's Store played in the early settlement of the area, the Virginia Department of Historic Resources erected an historical marker near the site of the old mercantile, at the front of the estate.

BREAKFAST BEVERAGES

In addition to freshly brewed coffee, one of these special drinks makes a great eye-opener!

PEACHY BUTTERMILK

2 cups lowfat buttermilk (or nonfat yogurt)
2 cups peeled, sliced peaches (peeled and sliced nectarines or mangos may be substituted)
1/2 cup frozen orange juice concentrate

Combine all ingredients in blender and process until smooth and frothy. Nice served with an orange wedge as garnish.
Yield: 2 servings.

ORANGE BREAKFAST NOG

1 cup skim milk
1/4 cup frozen orange juice concentrate, thawed and undiluted
1 tablespoon sugar
1 teaspoon vanilla extract
4 ice cubes
Strips of orange rind

Combine all ingredients in blender. Process until smooth and frothy. Garnish with strips of orange rind. Serve immediately.
Yield: 2 servings.

TROPICAL SHAKE

This drink makes me think of the wonderful fresh fruit drinks we enjoy while sailing in the Caribbean islands ... one sip and I'm back in that carefree environment!

> 2 frozen, peeled bananas
> 1 1/2 cups peeled, chopped mango (1 medium)
> 1 1/2 cups peeled, chopped papaya (1 medium)
> 1 tablespoon honey
> 2 teaspoons lime juice
> 1/2 teaspoon coconut flavoring
> 1 (12-ounce) can guava nectar
> 1 (6-ounce) can unsweetened pineapple juice
> Lime wedges and lime rind curls for garnish

Combine all ingredients in blender; process until smooth. Spoon into individual glasses. Garnish with lime wedges and rind curls.
Yield: 6 servings.

CHOCOLATE MOCHA

> 1 (8-ounce) carton coffee low fat yogurt
> 2 teaspoons unsweetened cocoa
> 2 tablespoons honey
> 2 cups skim milk
> 1/4 cup vanilla low fat yogurt

Place coffee yogurt in freezer; freeze 2 hours or until almost frozen. Combine cocoa and honey in a small bowl; add milk and stir well. Gently stir in coffee yogurt. To serve, pour 3/4 cup mixture into each of 4 serving glasses. Garnish each with 1 tablespoon vanilla yogurt and sprinkle with ground nutmeg.
Yield: 4 servings.

MANOR SUNRISE

This recipe was the creation of our multi-talented Assistant Innkeeper, Debbie Leatherman. It is most appropriate, as she typically rises before the sun in order to prepare a special breakfast for our guests ... so to say that she makes the "Sun rise at the Manor" is no exaggeration!

The effect of the drink is that of a sunrise ... with the gradations of color from rosy to sunshine yellow. Debbie garnishes the glasses with a fresh strawberry and an orange slice for extra elegance (presentation is one of her specialities!).

6 frozen, peeled bananas
1 cup nonfat plain yogurt
**2 cups orange juice (apple or pineapple juice can
   be used for a variation on this theme)**
1 tablespoon vanilla
1 tablespoon honey
Strawberry puree:
1/4 cup strawberry preserves
**2 cups fresh strawberries (or frozen, thawed,
   and drained)**

First, make the strawberry puree (it can be made ahead and refrigerated or even frozen for future use). Blenderize the strawberries and preserves until creamy and smooth. Set aside in a refrigerator-tight container.

In blender, combine bananas, yogurt, orange juice, vanilla, and honey. Process until creamy and smooth (hence the colloquial term "smoothie").

To serve, fill the glass (we serve in a 10-ounce wine goblet with "The Manor at Taylor's Store" logo on it) with 2 tablespoons of the strawberry puree and 6 ounces of the yogurt/banana mixture. Garnish a la Debbie ... with fresh strawberry and orange slice.

Yield: 8 servings.

TOUR OF THE MANOR: THE ENGLISH GARDEN SUITE

The English Garden Suite is the favorite of many of our regular guests...it's cozy, private, and accessible to hot tub and other activities. The private indoor sitting porch with antique wicker furnishings provides a comfortable spot to read, relax, and enjoy the views of the countryside.

Hanging on the wall behind the antique brass bed is a hand-stitched quilt. There is an inlaid walnut wardrobe where two thirsty terry cloth bathrobes hang waiting for guests to grab them on their way to the hot tub. The bathroom in this suite is the only place where the original 1820's slave-made brick foundation is visible. The diversity and comfort of this little room is that of a cozy English cottage garden.

HOT FRUITED CIDER

This hot drink is one of our favorites in the fall when the freshly pressed cider is available from the local orchards. The smell of it simmering on the stove is a nice welcome for guests when they arrive on a chilly fall afternoon, after a day of "leaf peeking" along the Blue Ridge Parkway.

1 quart freshly pressed apple cider
3 cups unsweetened pineapple-orange juice
1/4 cup firmly packed brown sugar
10 whole cloves
2 (3-inch) cinnamon sticks
Extra cinnamon sticks for garnish

Combine first 5 ingredients in a Dutch oven; bring to a boil. Cover, reduce heat, and simmer at least 5 minutes (it can stay on the stove on very low heat for several hours, if you are expecting company or having a holiday party). Strain; discard spices. Serve in mugs garnished with a cinnamon stick.

Yield: 8 servings.

BREAKFAST SOUPS

Soup for breakfast? How preposterous! These soups are an innovative way to commence the day ... and we feel that a day started in a unique and fun way will be a unique and fun day. Our offering unusual and delicious breakfasts sets the stage for that special experience for our B&B guests.

Try any of these soups for your next breakfast, brunch, or even dinner ... they're light, healthy, and delicious!

LAYERED CHERRY-BERRY SOUP

This soup is a special offering when our local cherries are available... but can be made year-round with canned cherries (drained of syrup) and frozen raspberries (thawed and drained).

        2 cups water
        1/4 cup sugar
        2 tablespoons cornstarch
        1/2 teaspoon cinnamon
        1 cup pitted fresh sweet cherries (about 1/3 pound)
        1 cup fresh raspberries
        1 (8-ounce) carton vanilla low fat yogurt

Combine first 4 ingredients in a medium non-aluminum saucepan; stir well. Add cherries and raspberries; place over medium heat, and bring to a boil, stirring frequently. Remove from heat, let cool.

Position knife blade in food processor bowl; add cherry mixture. Process 30 seconds. Stop processor; scrape sides of bowl with a rubber spatula. Process until smooth. Strain puree; discard seeds. Place cherry puree in a bowl; cover and chill.

Combine 1/2 cup cherry puree and low fat yogurt in a small bowl; stir well. Spoon 1/4 cup cherry-yogurt mixture into each of 4 small bowls; set aside remaining 2 tablespoons cherry-yogurt mixture. Spoon 1/2 cup remaining cherry puree evenly over each serving.

Divide remaining 2 tablespoons cherry-yogurt mixture evenly among servings by placing 1/4 teaspoon dollops in a circular pattern over cherry puree. Pull a toothpick through dollops to make a pattern. Chill.

Yield: 4 servings.

SANTA FE STYLE HONEYDEW SOUP

This recipe is reminiscent of my beloved Southwestern cuisine, a sweet dish with a slight spicy twinge. A very lovely presentation for this soup is to cut the melon in half and scoop out the flesh, then use the hollowed melon half as a serving bowl.

1 honeydew melon (6-7 pounds with 8-10 cups
    scooped out flesh)
2 teaspoons safflower oil
2 fresh jalapeno or serrano peppers
1/2 cup sweet white wine or white grape juice
2/3 cup fresh lime juice
2 tablespoons honey
1/4 teaspoon white pepper
Nonfat plain yogurt for serving
1/2 sweet red pepper, finely diced

Cut the melon in 1/2 and scoop out, then discard the seeds. With a spoon, scoop out the flesh. Set melon aside.

Heat safflower oil in a 2-quart saucepan over medium-high heat. Add the jalapenos and cook, stirring, until soft, about 3 minutes. Add the wine and bring the mixture to a boil. Remove from heat.

In a blender, whirl the melon pieces, jalapeno mixture, lime juice, honey and white pepper. Puree until smooth. Pour into a bowl. Cover and refrigerate until cold, at least 2 hours.

Serve in chilled bowls (or melon halves) with a dollop of yogurt and a sprinkle of finely diced red pepper.

Yield: Serves 8.

TOUR OF THE MANOR: ARTWORK

The artwork in the Parlor and throughout the first floor is primarily by local artists. Robert Shepherd, a Lynchburg artist, painted several paintings of the house and the surrounding estate for us. Ruth Cole, of Moneta, specializes in the Impressionist style still life which has an "old world" feel about it. Jane Stogner, of Ferrum, painted the magnificent landscape of the mountains of Franklin County which hangs in the sunporch. The needlepoint pillows and wallhangings are the handiwork of our own Nancy Crow and Debbie Leatherman. Combining antiques with special local pieces gives The Manor its own personality...the dignity of an elegant, loving grandmother.

CHILLED PINEAPPLE PEACH SOUP

2 cups peaches, peeled, pitted, sliced
1 can pineapple chunks (or 1/2 a fresh pineapple if
   a ripe one is available)
1 cup orange juice
1 cup pineapple juice
2 cups plain nonfat yogurt
1/2 cup dry white wine
1 tablespoon lemon juice
Lime wedges and mint for garnish

Puree peaches and pineapple in food processor until smooth. Add the juices, yogurt, and wine and blend well. Strain the soup through a fine sieve.

Serve chilled, garnished with thin slices of lime and mint leaves.

Yield: 8 servings.

JUST PEACHY SOUP

In late August, the Roanoke Farmer's Market is loaded with peaches from local orchards. This recipe takes full advantage of the fresh, sweet fruit!

1 cup peeled, sliced fresh peaches
1/4 cup apricot nectar
1/8 teaspoon nutmeg
1 (8-ounce) carton lowfat vanilla yogurt

Blend all ingredients together in food processor or blender until smooth, scraping sides of bowl with a rubber spatula. Cover and chill. Serve in chilled bowls with a sprinkle of nutmeg and mint sprig garnish.

Yield: 2 cups, 2 servings.

HEART HEALTHY VIRGINIA PEANUT SOUP

While this recipe isn't exactly a breakfast item, I couldn't leave it out of this cookbook. When Lee and I first started the B&B there were no restaurants in the Smith Mountain Lake area. So, rather than send our guests all the way into Roanoke for dinner...we decided to offer dinner meals as well as breakfast. Our original idea was just to have a simple "hearty soup and crusty bread" waiting for them on arrival ... but our adventurous nature quickly led us into offering a full six-course gourmet dinner. We had a wonderful time planning unusual meals and serving them to the appreciative diners ... whose accolades were a tremendous source of satisfaction. However, as our business grew ... and the Lake area grew with new restaurants ... we decided to concentrate on the B&B rather than developing a full scale restaurant.

This Virginia Peanut Soup was the traditional second course of our 6-course meal. We adapted the recipe from the old Virginia recipe to make it more heart healthy.

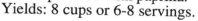

**2 ribs of celery, chopped
1 medium onion, chopped
2 tablespoons safflower margarine
2 tablespoons flour
2 cups chicken broth
2 cups skim milk
1 cup peanut butter (natural, freshly ground,
    without added oil, sugar, salt, or
    additives) either crunchy or smooth
Salt, pepper, paprika**

Brown celery and onions in margarine. Add flour and chicken broth and bring to a boil. Add milk and combine well, reduce heat to medium low. Add peanut butter (whisking helps it combine better) and simmer for 5 minutes.

Ladle the soup into a blender in small batches and blenderize until smooth. Return it to the pan, reheat and season with salt and pepper to taste.

Serve sprinkled with paprika.
Yields: 8 cups or 6-8 servings.

MOOSEWOOD CHOOSE-YOUR-OWN FRUIT SOUP

The mark of a good cookbook is that the pages are all wilted, dog-earred and stained with trails of ingredients across the favorite recipes. This bedraggled appearance bears testimony to the book's achievement of its purpose (I can only hope that your copy of this cookbook will one day attain that status!). The original "Moosewood Cookbook" by Mollie Katzen, published in 1977, is such a cookbook in my kitchen. Her "Enchanted Broccoli Forest" runs a close second in the frequency of use category ... wonderful vegetarian recipes and menu ideas. The soup recipes from both books are positively fool-proof and can be made for company without trying them out first (another mark of a good cookbook!).

This fruit soup recipe may be made with infinite variations, and is best suited to those of you who prefer to cook by taste rather than follow a strict recipe. (The preceding fruit soup recipes are better suited for the strict-recipe-type cooks ... we're all different!) Use what you have on hand, and get creative!

3 cups fruit juice (unsweetened - orange,
apple, pineapple, grape - your choice)
A banana
Chopped, peeled apple
1/2 teaspoon dried mint
Juice from 1 lemon
A chopped, peeled peach
Pieces of fresh cantaloupe
A couple tablespoons honey (to taste)
1 cup Yogurt or buttermilk
Dash of: cinnamon, nutmeg, allspice,
sweet wine - you choose

Blenderize all ingredients together. If you like it thick, add more bananas or yogurt. If you like it thin, add more fruit juice. Top each serving with yogurt ... or a violet ... or a rose. Heavenly!

Yield 4-6 servings.

TOUR OF THE MANOR: THE GREAT ROOM

The huge, brick fireplace with hand-hewn cedar mantel is the focal point of the gigantic slate-floored great room. This recreational room offers interesting activities for all guests. There is a billiard room on one end. The large screen TV and VCR provide guests entertainment with the classic movie collection. Chess, backgammon, and cards are available for fireside games.

Around the corner, there is a wet bar and an interesting antique "captain's sink" from an old ship. The adjacent guest kitchen provides guests with continuous coffee, tea, lemonade, and cookies, as well as refrigerator, microwave, and full cooking facilities for do-it-yourselves meals and snacks.

The exercise room is behind the guest kitchen, for those guests who want to keep up with their fitness programs while travelling. There is a cross-country ski machine, a rowing machine, an exercise bike, and a resistance weight trainer.

The hot tub is just outside the guest kitchen. Ideal for relaxing while stargazing and listening to favorite music...the hot tub is for all guests' use, but private while being used.

All of the activities and amenities offered in the great room, guest kitchen, and exercise room make The Manor unique among B&Bs and small inns.

BREAD BASKET

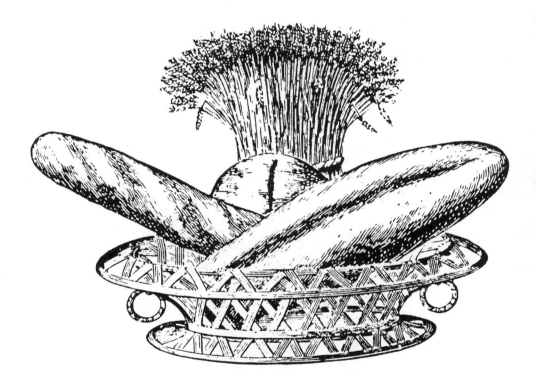

MUFFINS

Muffins are probably the one food most associated with the "B&B experience", and for good reasons. There are as many different varieties of muffins as there are B&Bs, and each has its own special qualities (like B&Bs). Moreover, each B&B innkeeper has his/her favorite muffin recipe that he/she swears is the "best in the world", bearing testimony to the marvelous spectrum of individuality in the muffin kingdom (and the B&B kingdom!).

The muffin recipes we've included here were selected by a process of sampling and rating conducted by all of our B&B staff. The prerequisite for testing was that the recipe be modified for a lower fat content and preferably high in fiber (either bran or whole wheat flour). We combined recipes, added and subtracted ingredients, and each made suggestions for improvements before determining which recipes to include in this cookbook.

Here are the winners!

OAT BRAN MUFFINS

Our dear friends, Laura and Greg Trafidlo, are professional musicians with 4 albums and nationwide concerts to their credit. Laura and I knew each other in our "former lives" as nurses, and our relationship added a new dimension when she and Greg were married at Taylor's Store. One of their most popular songs echoes (humorously) our sentiments about the benefits of healthful eating.

"OAT BRAN MUFFINS"
by Steve Key
As performed by Laura Pole and Greg Trafidlo

"Honey brew up some coffee, I got a new treat for you.
It's gonna make our lovin' last,
Our hearts will beat like new.
It's oat bran muffins, put 'em in the oven
For life long lovin' ... oat bran muffins.
Well, I used to be a
Ham and cheese omelet girl,
With a bagel and cream cheese, too
But if you want to have fun past thirty-one,
Then you gotta make a change or two.
So toss out that tub of butter,
T-bone steak and eggs
Whip up the bran and the egg-beaters
Honey don't make me beg ...
Now, honey I know that a muffin alone
Won't keep the doctor away
So here's my solution,
Let's join that revolution
And we'll start a "bran" new day!
We'll start with oat bran crunch for breakfast,
Then it's oat bran bread at noon,
We'll have tofu meatless loaf,
And a bathroom built for two!"

OAT BRAN MUFFINS

1 cup oat bran
1 1/4 cups whole wheat pastry flour
1/3 cup brown sugar
2 1/2 teaspoons baking powder
1/4 teaspoon baking soda
1/4 teaspoon nutmeg
1/4 teaspoon cinnamon
1 cup lowfat buttermilk
1 teaspoon vanilla
2 egg whites (or 1/4 cup egg substitute)
2 tablespoons canola oil
3/4 cup shredded apple (for a variation,
    you may use shredded carrots instead)

Combine first 7 ingredients. Set aside. Combine milk, vanilla, egg whites, and oil. Make well in dry ingredients and add wet ingredients. Stir until just combined. Stir in apple.

Spray muffin tins and fill them with batter 2/3 full. Bake at 375° for 18-20 minutes.

This batter can be made ahead and stored in an airtight container in the refrigerator for up to 5 days.

Yield: 12 large muffins.

TOUR OF THE MANOR: THE PLANTATION SUITE

There are six working fireplaces in The Manor, the only one in a guest room is in the Plantation Suite. Painted "hunt green" and decorated with rich fabrics that lend the feeling of plantation opulence, it is one of the most popular guest rooms. The two double, half-tester canopied beds are both antiques, from a plantation in Buckingham County, Virginia. Both of walnut, one was handmade on that plantation.

The Queen Anne tilt-top table in the corner was built around 1770 of walnut. The dresser is a transition piece from the late Empire period to early Victorian era, circa 1850. Perhaps one of the most interesting features in the Plantation Suite is the chandelier. Handmade by a New England craftsman to replicate an early colonial fixture, it has no visible electrical wiring and even has candles hand-dipped in beeswax.

The room itself has an interesting history as well. For the Price family, who lived in The Manor from 1876-1950, it was the bedroom of the matriarch, Elizabeth Ferguson Price. Family members have told us that at least 13 babies were born in that room! Grown daughters would "come home" to have their children, and the area that is now the dressing room served as a nursery. No wonder the room has such a joyful atmosphere!

LEMON YOGURT MUFFINS

These delightful muffins are requested by several of our favorite guests on their return visits. Their sweet, but tart, nature makes them the perfect compliment to a savory breakfast dish such as Manor Potatoes.

1 cup whole wheat pastry flour
1 cup all-purpose flour
1 teaspoon baking powder
1 teaspoon baking soda
1/4 teaspoon salt
1/4 cup sugar
2 tablespoons honey
1/2 cup egg substitute
1 1/4 cups nonfat plain yogurt
1/4 cup margarine, melted
1 tablespoon grated lemon zest
Lemon syrup:
1/3 cup lemon juice
1/3 cup sugar
3 tablespoons water

Preheat the oven to 375° and spray muffin tins with cooking spray. In a small mixing bowl, stir and toss together the flour, baking powder, baking soda, and salt. In another, larger bowl, combine the sugar, honey, eggs, yogurt, melted margarine, and lemon zest and beat until thoroughly mixed. Add the combined dry ingredients and beat until just blended.

Spoon the batter into the prepared muffin tins, filling about 2/3 full. Bake for about 15 minutes, or until the tops are delicately browned and a toothpick inserted into center of a muffin comes out clean.

While the muffins bake, prepare the syrup. Combine the lemon juice, sugar, and water in a small saucepan. Bring to boil, boil for 1 minute, then set aside.

When muffins are done, remove the pan from the oven and gently poke the top of each muffin two or three times with a fork. Drizzle about 2 teaspoons of the syrup over each hot muffin, letting it run over the top and around the edge. Let cool in the pans for a few minutes, then remove and serve warm.

Yield: 1 dozen large or 3 dozen mini-muffins.

THE BEST BLUEBERRY MUFFINS

In our "family" test kitchen ... this recipe was the most popular. Fresh blueberries are wonderful, when you can get them, but the frozen, unsweetened berries work fine.

1 1/2 cups all-purpose flour
1/4 cup sugar
1 1/2 teaspoons baking powder
1/4 teaspoon salt
2 egg whites (1/4 cup egg substitute)
2/3 cup orange juice
2 tablespoons canola oil
1 teaspoon vanilla
1 cup fresh or frozen blueberries

In a medium mixing bowl combine flour, sugar, baking powder, and salt. In a small mixing bowl beat egg whites, orange juice, oil, and vanilla. Add to dry ingredients, stirring just until moistened. Fold in blueberries.

Spray muffin tins with cooking spray (we use the mini-muffin tins for this). Fill cups half full of batter. Bake at 400° for 15-17 minutes, or until golden brown. Cool before serving.

Yield: 36 mini-muffins.

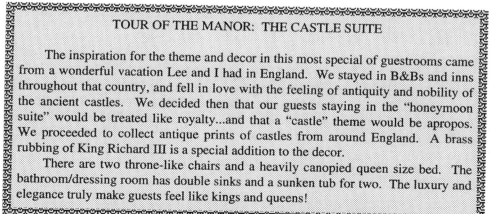

TOUR OF THE MANOR: THE CASTLE SUITE

The inspiration for the theme and decor in this most special of guestrooms came from a wonderful vacation Lee and I had in England. We stayed in B&Bs and inns throughout that country, and fell in love with the feeling of antiquity and nobility of the ancient castles. We decided then that our guests staying in the "honeymoon suite" would be treated like royalty...and that a "castle" theme would be apropos. We proceeded to collect antique prints of castles from around England. A brass rubbing of King Richard III is a special addition to the decor.

There are two throne-like chairs and a heavily canopied queen size bed. The bathroom/dressing room has double sinks and a sunken tub for two. The luxury and elegance truly make guests feel like kings and queens!

CRANBERRY OATMEAL MUFFINS

The crunchy texture and rich flavor of these muffins won points with the "muffin judges"! Try them with one of the Turkey Sausage recipes for a Thanksgiving breakfast.

1 1/2 cups all-purpose flour
1 tablespoon baking powder
3/4 teaspoon salt
1/4 cup walnuts, finely chopped
1/2 cup dried cranberries (or dark, seedless raisins)
3/4 cup oats
2 tablespoons canola oil
3/4 cup firmly packed light brown sugar
3/4 cup lowfat buttermilk
1/4 cup egg substitute

Preheat oven to 350°. Spray muffin tins with cooking spray. Whisk together flour, baking powder, and salt in a large bowl. Toss nuts and cranberries with 1 teaspoon of flour mixture in small bowl. Set aside. Stir oats into remaining flour mixture.

Beat together oil, sugar, buttermilk, and egg substitute in a bowl until all ingredients are smooth and blended. Add this mixture to flour mixture, stirring together all ingredients just until everything is evenly moistened. Fold in nut-cranberry mixture. Fill muffin tin cups 2/3 full.

Bake at 350° for 12-15 minutes, or until wooden pick inserted comes out clean. Cool muffins in pan on wire rack for 5 minutes, then turn them out onto rack.

Yield: 16 muffins.

REFRIGERATOR BRAN MUFFINS

This is a variation of a muffin that is very popular with innkeepers because the batter is made up ahead and stored in the refrigerator for up to 2 weeks. Fresh muffins every morning ... with most of the preparation done ahead. We like to add freshly chopped apples, pears, or nuts before baking.

2 cups all bran cereal
1 1/2 cups lowfat buttermilk
2 cups all-purpose flour
1/2 cup whole wheat flour
1 cup sugar
1 teaspoon baking powder
1 teaspoon baking soda
1 teaspoon cinnamon
1 teaspoon ginger
1/4 teaspoon salt
1/2 cup raisins
1 cup unsweetened applesauce
1/2 cup canola oil
1/2 cup egg substitute

In medium bowl, combine cereal and buttermilk; let stand 5 minutes or until cereal is softened. In a large bowl, combine flours, sugar, baking powder, baking soda, cinnamon, ginger, salt, and raisins; mix well. To cereal mixture, add applesauce, oil, and egg substitute; blend well. Add to dry ingredients all at once; stir just until dry ingredients are moistened.

This batter can be baked immediately or stored for up to 2 weeks in an airtight container in refrigerator.

When ready to bake, spray muffin tins with cooking spray and fill 2/3 full with batter. Bake at 400° for 15-20 minutes or until toothpick inserted in center comes out clean. Immediately remove from pan; serve warm.

Yield: 30 muffins.

HARVEST MUFFINS

These are my personal favorite ... dense and flavorful, with the addition of pumpkin, carrots, and zucchini.

2 cups all-purpose flour
1 cup rolled oats
3/4 cup firmly packed brown sugar
3 teaspoons baking powder
1/2 teaspoon cinnamon
1/4 teaspoon salt
2/3 cup skim milk
1/4 cup canned pumpkin
1/4 cup egg substitute
1 cup finely shredded carrot
1/2 cup shredded unpeeled zucchini (1 small)
1/2 cup walnuts, chopped

Preheat oven to 400°. Spray 12 muffin cups with cooking spray. In large bowl, combine flour, oats, brown sugar, baking powder, cinnamon, and salt; mix well. In a small bowl, combine milk, oil, and egg substitute; blend well. Add to dry ingredients all at once; stir just until dry ingredients are moistened. Stir in carrot and zucchini just until blended. Spoon batter into muffin tin.

Bake at 400° for 16-20 minutes or until golden brown and toothpick inserted in center comes out clean. Immediately remove from pan; serve warm.

Yield: 12 muffins.

TOUR OF THE MANOR: THE VICTORIAN ROOM

The first of our B&B rooms to be completed, the Victorian Room is a source of special pride for Lee and me. As with the entire renovation/decoration of the inn, we worked together on everything from selection of fabrics to furnishings. We also did all of the painting ourselves, and had a particularly memorable experience getting the shade of "rose" just right for the Victorian Room.

The walnut Victorian bed (c. 1870) is absolutely beautiful, and incidentally is very much like the one which Robert E. Lee slept in when he was President of Washington College in Lexington (now Washington and Lee University). The tapestry-upholstered rosewood chairs were from the local estate of Minnie Jones (mentioned in the parlor tour)...with the original upholstery still in service. The lovely tapestries hanging on the walls were from the French exhibition at the New Orleans Worlds Fair. The gorgeous balloon shade curtains were made by our dear friend, Jean Loughry (who actually made all of the draperies and bed hangings throughout The Manor). All go together to create a very Victorian ambience.

APPLESAUCE OATMEAL MUFFINS

These yummy muffins are ideal for afternoon tea!

1 cup all-purpose flour
1 cup whole wheat flour
1 cup sugar
4 teaspoons baking powder
1 1/2 teaspoons salt
1 1/2 teaspoons cinnamon
1/2 teaspoon nutmeg
Pinch ground clove
2 cups applesauce
1/2 cup melted margarine
3/4 cup egg substitute
1 1/2 cups plus 2 tablespoons oats
1 cup raisins

Preheat oven to 375°. Spray 36 mini-muffin tins with cooking spray. Combine flour, sugar, baking powder, salt, cinnamon, nutmeg, and cloves in large bowl. Combine applesauce, margarine, and egg substitute in medium bowl. Stir into dry ingredients until moistened. Stir in the 1 1/2 cups oats and the raisins.

Spoon batter into prepared muffin cups. Sprinkle tops with remaining oats. Bake 10-15 minutes or until toothpick inserted in the center comes out clean. Remove from pans.

Yield: 36 mini-muffins.

HOLLADAY HOUSE APPLE MUFFINS

Our friends, Phebe and Pete Holladay are innkeepers in Orange, Virginia. Their B&B is in a home that has been in their family for over 100 years, and their warmth and hospitality make guests feel like one of the family. This recipe won the Holladays the "Best Muffin in Virginia" award at the 1994 Bed and Breakfast Association of Virginia Conference.

1 cup lowfat buttermilk
1 teaspoon salt
1 teaspoon baking soda
1 teaspoon vanilla
1 1/2 cups brown sugar
1 egg
2/3 cup oil
2 cups all-purpose flour, sifted
1 1/2 cups chopped apple
1/2 cup chopped pecans

Combine the first four ingredients. In a separate bowl, combine the brown sugar, egg, and oil and mix. Then, blend the two mixtures together. Add the flour and mix until all ingredients are moistened. Add the apples and pecans and distribute them throughout. Spray muffin tins and fill. Bake at 350° for 30 minutes.

Yield: 1 dozen muffins.

THE SPLIT-RAIL FENCE

Many of our guests are curious about the split-rail fence encircling the front pasture of the estate. "Has that fence been there since the 1800's?", they want to know. Well, there was indeed a split-rail fence, in that style, around that pasture until the early part of the 20th century. The fence now in place was Lee's handiwork, however. Keeping the exterior appearance of the Manor and the grounds as "period appropriate" as possible has always been one of our guiding tenets, and when it came to fencing the property in front of the Manor, we wanted it to look like it would have looked in the 1800's.

We advertised locally and found farmers who had old chestnut-rail fences fallen into disuse on their properties. We rummaged around several farms and were able to find enough of the original 200 year old chestnut logs to do the job (their authenticity is testified to by the fact that the American Chestnut tree has been extinct for over 100 years).

Lee studied the various styles of split-rail fences to determine which would have been used in this part of the country, then proceeded to construct the fence...even dressed in period clothing (pioneer shirt and leather vest)!

Each project around the Manor has been an educational and fun experience for us...and has brought a new dimension of interest and authenticity to the historic property.

MRS. BELL'S SCOTTISH SCONES

My grandmother's next door neighbor for over 40 years was a woman who immigrated as a young girl from Scotland. "Mrs" Bell (they never referred to each other by first name) was considerably older than my grandmother and taught her many of the "Old Country" ways to do things, such as keeping house, stitching, disciplining children, and how to make these genuine Scottish scones. They have become a family favorite. My grandfather and uncle would go to great lengths to get a batch for "tea time" in the afternoon!

2 **cups unbleached flour**
2 **teaspoons baking powder**
1/2 **teaspoon salt**
1/4 **teaspoon baking soda**
6 **tablespoons margarine (or splurge and use butter)**
1/2 **cup raisins**
1/2 **cup lowfat buttermilk**
1 **large egg**
1 **tablespoon milk**
1 **tablespoon sugar**

Preheat oven to 425°. Lightly grease a baking sheet. In a large bowl, combine the flour, baking powder, salt and baking soda. With a pastry blender, cut in the margarine until the mixture resembles coarse crumbs. Mix in the raisins with a fork.

In a cup, beat together the buttermilk and egg, then add them to the flour mixture. Mix lightly with a fork until the mixture clings together and forms a ball of soft dough. Turn the dough onto a lightly floured surface and knead gently, turning 5-6 times. Cut dough in half and form it into 2 large balls, then with a floured rolling pin, roll the dough to 1/2-inch thickness, keeping the circular shape to the dough. Cut each of the dough circles with a floured knife into 8 wedges. Place the scones 1 inch apart on the greased baking sheet. Lightly brush the tops of the scones with milk and sprinkle with sugar. Bake 10-12 minutes or until golden brown

Yield: 16 scones.

APRICOT-OAT BRAN SCONES

1 1/2 cups unbleached flour
1 cup oat bran
2 tablespoons sugar
1 tablespoon baking powder
1/2 teaspoon salt
1/2 cup margarine
3 tablespoons milk
1 egg
1 (17-ounce) can apricot halves, drained & chopped

Combine flour, oat bran, sugar, baking powder and salt. Cut in margarine until mixture becomes fine crumbs. Add egg, milk and apricots and stir just until dough leaves side of bowl. Divide dough in half; turn onto lightly floured surface. Roll or pat each portion of dough into a 6-inch circle that's 1-inch thick. Use a floured knife to cut each round into 6 wedges. Place on ungreased baking sheet. Bake in 400° oven for 12 minutes or until golden brown.

Yield: 12 scones.

WHOLE WHEAT RAISIN SCONES

1 cup unbleached flour
1 cup stone-ground whole wheat flour
1/2 cup miller's bran
2 teaspoons baking powder
1/2 teaspoon baking soda
1/2 teaspoon nutmeg
1/2 teaspoon salt
1 stick margarine
1 cup raisins
2 tablespoons granulated sugar
1 egg yolk
3/4 cup lowfat buttermilk or nonfat plain yogurt
1 egg white
Additional sugar for sprinkling

Heat oven to 375°. Put flour, baking powder, baking soda, nutmeg, and salt into a large bowl; stir to mix well. Add butter and cut in with a pastry blender or rub in with your fingers, until the mixture looks like fine granules. Add raisins and sugar; toss to distribute evenly.

Add egg yolk to buttermilk/yogurt in a measuring cup and whisk with a fork to blend. Pour over the flour mixture and stir with a fork until a soft dough forms.

Turn out dough onto a lightly floured surface and give 10-12 kneads. Cut dough in half. Knead each half briefly into a ball; turn smooth side up and pat dough into a 6-inch circle. Cut into 6 wedges, but do not separate wedges. In a small bowl, beat the egg white with a fork until just broken up. Brush the top of each scone with egg white and sprinkle lightly with sugar. With a spatula, carefully transfer the two cut circles to an ungreased cookie sheet. If necessary, reshape the circles so that the 6 wedges are touching (this will keep the raisins from burning).

Bake 18-22 minutes, until golden brown. Cool on wire rack; after 5 minutes pull wedges apart and cover loosely with a dish towel.

Yield: 12 scones.

BISCUITS

Biscuits are synonymous with a Southern breakfast. Biscuits with gravy, biscuits with ham, biscuits with butter and honey... the scent of freshly baked biscuits wafting through gingham curtains across the farmyard beckoning the hungry indoors for a hearty breakfast after early morning chores. The same delectable aroma summons our B&B guests into the dining room when we bake these traditional Southern biscuits.

Agatha Dudley was the first staff person to join us when the B&B business began to grow and we were no longer able to do it all ourselves. She loves the guests, and they love her. She enjoys sharing her life-long knowledge of Franklin County, her genuine interest in and concern for others, and her optimistic and uplifting philosophy of life. Her traditional Virginia biscuits are a special treat that brighten the morning as much as her cheerful "Good Morning!".

AGATHA'S TRADITIONAL VIRGINIA BISCUITS

**2 cups self-rising flour (or 2 cups all-purpose flour
with 1 teaspoon baking powder and
1/2 teaspoon salt added)
1/2 cup vegetable oil (or margarine)
1 cup lowfat buttermilk**

Combine all ingredients in a large bowl and work together using a fork. Turn dough out onto a lightly floured surface; knead 3-4 times. Roll dough to 3/4-inch thickness; cut with biscuit cutter and place on a baking sheet. Bake at 425° for 12-14 minutes, or until golden brown.

Yield: 12 biscuits.

LIGHT & EASY BISCUITS

2 cups flour
1 tablespoon baking powder
1/4 teaspoon baking soda
1/2 teaspoon salt
1/4 cup margarine
1 (8-ounce) carton nonfat plain yogurt
1 teaspoon honey

Combine first 4 ingredients in bowl. Cut in margarine with a pastry blender until mixture resembles coarse meal. Add remaining ingredients and stir until just moistened.

Turn dough out onto floured surface and knead lightly 4-5 times. Roll dough to 1/2-inch thickness. Cut biscuits with a 2-inch cutter. Place on ungreased baking sheet. Bake at 425° for 10-12 minutes (until golden brown).

Yield: 2 dozen biscuits.

WHOLE WHEAT BISCUITS

1 cup white flour
1/2 cup whole wheat flour
2 tablespoons sugar
2 1/2 teaspoons baking powder
1/2 teaspoon salt
1/2 cup skim milk
3 tablespoons canola oil

Combine first 5 ingredients. Make well in mixture. Combine milk and oil; stir into dry ingredients until just moistened. Turn dough out onto lightly floured surface. Knead 3-4 times. Roll to 1/2-inch thickness; cut with 2 1/2-inch cutter. Bake on ungreased baking sheet at 400° for 12-15 minutes.

Yield: 8-10 biscuits.

OATMEAL DROP BISCUITS

1 1/4 cups unbleached flour
1 1/2 teaspoons baking powder
1/2 teaspoon salt
3 tablespoons margarine, cut into 3 pieces and chilled
1 1/4 cups uncooked oatmeal
1/2 cup skim milk
3 tablespoons honey
1 egg
Cooking spray

Position knife blade in processor bowl; add first 4 ingredients. Process 10 seconds or until mixture resembles coarse meal. Add oats; process 5 seconds. Combine milk, honey, and egg; add to flour mixture. Process 5 seconds or just until dry ingredients are moist.

Drop dough by rounded tablespoonfuls onto a baking sheet coated with cooking spray. Bake at 425° for 8 minutes.

Yield: 16 biscuits (with a rough, uneven top).

THE GOOSE PATROL

Guests taking a walk to the ponds are forewarned that they will be greeted by our resident gaggle of geese. While they are not meanly aggressive, they do aggressively pursue the handouts of goose feed presented to them...a source of surprise and amusement to most of our guests.

We ordered our first gaggle from the Sears catalog. They arrived at the post office, two days old, in a large box with little holes around it. The curious postmistress phoned to tell us, "You have a package here that is 'peeping' for water". We raised the goslings in the smokehouse, under a heat lamp, and as they got old enough we played "Father and Mother Goose" as they followed us around the lawn. At three months, they followed us down to the ponds and made themselves at home in their own little goose paradise.

Unfortunately, that little flock only lived two years before some type of predator had them for lunch. We had so appreciated their contribution to weed control, that we adopted the current flock from a retiring farmer.

This farmer lived on a rural lane, with a pond across the road from his house. Every evening, the geese would cross the road to the farmhouse, where he would generously feed them. Their first day at our ponds, about sunset, we received a phone call from one of our neighbors, "Are these your geese walking along the yellow line on the highway?"! From that point on, we have been conscientious about feeding them down at the ponds.

MARK'S WALNUT COFFEE CAKE

To quote our wonderful guest, Mark, who sent us this recipe after his visit in 1990, "As we said in parting, we certainly enjoyed our all-too-brief stay in your marvelous house. We will return with friends. Thanks again for your hospitality! I promised a recipe; it follows ... it will win you no end of kudos!". It's true (all of it).

1 1/2 cups unbleached flour
2 teaspoons baking powder
1/2 teaspoon salt
3/4 cup brown sugar
1/4 cup margarine or butter
1/2 cup milk
2 unbeaten eggs

Sift flour with baking powder and salt, and blend in sugar. Add margarine and milk and beat 300 strokes. Add eggs and beat 2 minutes.

Topping:
2 tablespoons melted butter
1/2 cup brown sugar
1 cup walnuts, chopped coarsely
1 tablespoon flour
1 teaspoon cinnamon

Combine butter, sugar, and walnuts with flour and cinnamon. Mix well. (Mark says: "I use a Bundt pan...the recipe says to use a 9-inch square ... either works fine.") Spread 1/2 of batter on bottom of greased pan and cover with 1/2 of topping. Repeat. Bake at 350° 30-35 minutes.

ARE THERE GHOSTS IN THE MANOR?

The first night that Lee and I spent in The Manor was a very memorable one. We had a mattress, an alarm clock, and a coffee pot...and we were camped out on the floor. After we turned out the lights and lay there contemplating the marvelous project before us...we were startled by a loud "thump, thump, thump", like a rapid knocking on the ceiling. This noise was repeated throughout the sleepless night. We were laughing to keep from being scared that we had actually purchased a haunted house!

Upon awaking, we realized that the "thump, thump, thump" continued into the daylight...followed the sound...and realized that the black walnut tree off of the back porch was dropping its ripe nuts onto the tin roof. The nuts were hitting the roof and loudly bouncing their way down.

Some guests are disappointed that that is the only haunting episode we've had at The Manor!

APPLE COFFEE CAKE

What does a fall morning smell like? The cinnamon and apples baking in this rich-tasting coffee cake! Makes you want to jump up to get outside and rake leaves!

4 cups unpeeled, finely diced cooking apples
1/2 cup orange juice, divided
1 1/2 teaspoons cinnamon
1/4 cup skim milk
1/2 cup margarine, softened
1 cup sugar
1 cup egg substitute
2 1/2 teaspoons vanilla extract
1 1/2 cups all-purpose flour
1 1/2 cups whole wheat flour
2 teaspoons baking powder
1/4 teaspoon salt
2 tablespoons brown sugar

Combine apple, 1/4 cup orange juice, and cinnamon in a medium bowl; stir well, and set aside. Combine remaining 1/4 cup orange juice and milk; stir well, and set aside.

Cream margarine; gradually add 1 cup sugar, beating at medium speed of an electric mixer until light and fluffy. Add egg substitute and vanilla; beat well.

Combine flours, baking powder, and salt, stirring well. Gradually add flour mixture to creamed mixture alternately with milk mixture, beginning and ending with flour mixture.

Pour half of batter into a 10-inch tube pan coated with cooking spray; top with half of apple mixture. Pour remaining batter into pan; top with remaining apple mixture, and sprinkle with brown sugar.

Bake at 350° for 1 hour and 10 minutes, or until cake springs back when lightly touched. Cool in pan on wire rack 10 minutes; unmold and cool completely.

Yield: 16 servings.
Fat: 6 gm Cholesterol: 0

NOT-REALLY-SOUR-CREAM PECAN COFFEE CAKE

This coffee cake is every bit as rich and delicious as traditional recipes for sour cream coffee cake, with much less fat!

1 cup sugar
1/4 cup vegetable oil
1 tablespoon minced lemon zest
1/2 cup egg substitute
1/2 cup non-fat, plain yogurt
1/2 cup lowfat cottage cheese
2 1/2 teaspoons vanilla extract
2 teaspoons fresh lemon juice
1 cup all-purpose flour
1 cup whole wheat pastry flour
4 tablespoons brown sugar
1/2 cup chopped pecans
1/2 teaspoon nutmeg
1 1/2 teaspoons cinnamon

Preheat oven to 350°. In a large bowl, cream the sugar, oil, and lemon zest. Add the egg substitute and mix completely. In a blender, process the yogurt and cottage cheese together until smooth and creamy. Add this mixture to the sugar/egg mixture. Add the vanilla and lemon juice and combine.

Sift together the baking powder and flours. Add this mixture gradually to batter, blending well.

Spray a 10-inch Bundt pan with cooking spray, then lightly dust with flour. In a small bowl, combine the nuts, brown sugar, nutmeg, and cinnamon. Spoon 1/3 of the batter into the pan, then 1/2 of the nut mixture, then 1/3 the batter, then remaining nuts, then remaining batter. Bake at 350° for 40-45 minutes, or until a toothpick inserted in cake comes out clean.

Yield: 24 slices.

ZUCCHINI LOAF

We have intentionally planted the gardens at The Manor with flowers, shrubs, herbs, and plants that would be appropriate to the 18-19th Century motif. We do not plant a vegetable garden (except for a few tomato plants ... there's NOTHING like a garden-ripe tomato). We found that when the vegetables are ripe in our area, they are so plentiful that friends are begging us to take some of them. Zucchini is one of those vegetables ... easy to grow ... and very prolific. In late June, we gratefully accept any and all zucchini donations... grate them in the food processor ... drain as much liquid as possible from the zucchini shreds ... and freeze them for multiple uses throughout the year. I LOVE zucchini-burgers (ask me for the recipe ... I'm not including it in this cookbook) ... and zucchini bread and muffins are always delicious.

1 cup coarsely shredded zucchini
2/3 cup sugar
1/2 cup skim milk
1/4 cup vegetable oil
1 egg, beaten (or 1/4 cup egg substitute)
1 1/4 cups all-purpose flour
1/2 cup whole wheat flour
1 teaspoon baking soda
1/4 teaspoon baking powder
1/2 teaspoon salt
1/2 teaspoon cinnamon
1 teaspoon vanilla
Cooking spray

Combine first 5 ingredients in a large bowl. Combine flour and next 5 ingredients; add to zucchini mixture, stirring just until dry ingredients are moistened. Stir in vanilla.

Pour batter into an 8-1/2x4-1/2x3-inch loaf pan coated with cooking spray; bake at 350° for 55 minutes or until a toothpick inserted in center comes out clean. Cool 15 minutes in pan on a wire rack; remove from pan, and cool on wire rack.

Yield: 16 servings.

VEGETABLE BREAKFAST LOAF

The vegetables and spices in this loaf make it equally delicious for a light summer supper, as an accompaniment to a big salad. For breakfast, a hearty slice served with fresh fruit and the Canadian Bacon with Currant Glaze makes a lovely meal.

1 medium onion, chopped
2 cloves garlic, minced
1 teaspoon olive oil
1/2 cup yellow bell pepper, chopped
1/2 cup red bell pepper, chopped
1/2 cup broccoli, finely chopped
1/2 cup shredded carrot
1 cup fresh corn kernels (frozen, thawed is okay)
1/2 cup finely chopped fresh parsley
1 tablespoon finely or 1 teaspoon dried herbs of
    your choice - I like summer savory or thyme - or
    we'll use a pre-mixed herb blend
1/2 teaspoon salt
1/4 teaspoon black pepper
1 cup all-purpose flour
1 cup whole wheat pastry flour
1 tablespoon baking powder
1 teaspoon baking soda
3/4 cup lowfat buttermilk
1/4 cup egg substitute
1/4 cup freshly grated Parmesan

Preheat oven to 375°. Lightly spray 8x11-inch baking dish with cooking spray. In a large skillet, sauté the onions and garlic over medium heat for two minutes, then add peppers and cook another 5 minutes. Next, add broccoli, carrots, and corn then cook another two minutes (you want the vegetables to still be crunchy, but softened). Turn off heat, add parsley, herb, salt, and pepper and allow this mixture to cool.

In a large bowl, sift together the flour, baking powder, and baking soda. Whisk in the buttermilk and egg substitute until just combined. Fold in the cooked vegetable mixture.

Spread the dough into the prepared pan. Bake at 375° for 20 minutes. Remove from oven, sprinkle with Parmesan cheese, return to oven and bake for another 30 minutes or until toothpick inserted comes out clean. Cool in pan on wire rack. Slice in half lengthwise, then again into 6 2-inch slices.

Yield: 12 hearty servings.

IRISH SODA BREAD

While travelling "B&B" through Ireland, I developed a love of this simple farmhouse bread, along with a love for the verdant, rolling countryside and the warm, cheerful Irish people. One bite of this light loaf brings back the image of breakfast at an ancient wide-plank dining table in a thatched-roof stone cottage in County Galway!

> 4 1/2 cups all-purpose flour
> 3 tablespoons plus 1 teaspoon sugar
> 1 tablespoon caraway seeds
> 4 teaspoons baking powder
> 1/2 teaspoon baking soda
> 1 teaspoon salt
> 1 cup dried currants, or dark seedless raisins
> 2 cups lowfat buttermilk

Heat the oven to 350°. Spray with cooking spray and flour a 9-inch cast-iron skillet. In a large bowl, mix 4 cups flour, 3 tablespoons sugar, caraway seeds, baking powder, baking soda, and salt. Stir in the currants, making sure they are separated. Add the buttermilk and mix with a fork to form a soft dough. Sprinkle about 1/4 cup of the remaining flour on a work surface, turn the dough out, and knead it until it is smooth, about 5 minutes. Use only as much of the remaining flour as needed to prevent the dough from sticking. Shape the dough into a smooth, round loaf and press it into prepared skillet. With a very sharp knife, cut a cross 1/2-inch deep across the top of the dough.

Bake the loaf 1 hour, or until lightly browned. It will sound hollow when it is tapped on the top. Remove the bread from the skillet. Rub the top with butter and sprinkle it with 1 teaspoon sugar. Cool it on a wire rack.

Yield: 1 loaf.

COLONIAL BROWN BREAD

Early settlers were very resourceful when it came to cooking. In remote areas, such as Franklin County, a family like the Booths would have had to rely on grains grown and milled locally, along with meat, produce, dairy, and eggs from their own farm. A few staple items could have been purchased at Taylor's Store and used creatively with these home-grown foods. It was discovered by Colonists that baking soda mixed with cornmeal, rye, and wheat flours would yield a reasonably light loaf of bread. Traditionally known as "Boston Brown Bread", this wholesome loaf is steamed and delicious served hot for breakfast (or with Boston Baked Beans for dinner!).

1 cup yellow cornmeal
1 cup rye flour
1 cup stone-ground whole wheat flour
2 teaspoons baking soda
1 teaspoon salt
2 cups lowfat buttermilk
3/4 cup dark molasses
3/4 cup dark, seedless raisins

Spray two empty one-pound metal coffee cans with cooking spray. In a large bowl, combine the cornmeal, flours, baking soda, and salt. In another large bowl, with an electric mixer on medium speed, beat the buttermilk and molasses until they are well blended. Add the flour mixture gradually, beating well after each addition. Stir in the raisins. Spoon the batter evenly into the greased coffee cans. Cover each with a piece of waxed paper sprayed with cooking spray, then the plastic coffee can lid.

In a large pot, boil enough water to reach half way up the sides of the cans. Put a wire rack in the pot and place cans on top of the rack. Over high heat, return the water to boiling. Reduce to low heat; cover pot and simmer 2 1/4 hours, adding more boiling water if needed to keep it at a halfway mark on the cans.

Bread may be turned out onto cutting board for immediate serving, or may be refrigerated in the covered can for up to 1 week. If refrigerated, reheat by steaming as above for about 30 minutes.

Yield: 2 loaves.

HOLIDAY FRUIT BREAD

Holiday season is very special at The Manor. The inn is decorated lavishly with fresh green wreaths; pine roping; a single candle in every window; an arrangement of fresh pineapple, apples, and magnolia leaves over the front door; and a beautiful Victorian Christmas tree on the sunporch. We do have guests come to visit for weekends during the month of December, to get away from the hustle bustle of the season at home, but generally December is rather quiet around the inn. It gives us the chance to do those little "extra" things that make the holidays really special, such as baking goodies to take to friends and neighbors. This recipe for Fruit Bread is one of my favorites. Unlike traditional fruit cake recipes, which call for the ultra-sweet, artificially colored candied fruit, this recipe relies on the natural sweetness of dried fruits. Any dried fruit will work ... try your favorites.

1 cup dried Calimyrna figs
1 cup dried apricots
1 cup golden raisins
1 1/2 cups water
1 cup pitted dates
1/4 cup margarine
3/4 cup sugar
1 egg
1 teaspoon grated lemon zest
1 cup all-purpose flour
1 cup whole wheat pastry flour
2 teaspoons baking powder
1 teaspoon baking soda
1 teaspoon salt

Preheat oven to 350°. Spray two loaf pans with cooking spray. Put the figs, apricots, and raisins in a small saucepan and add the water. Cover and simmer for 5 minutes. Drain, reserving 2/3 cup liquid. Cool. Chop the figs, apricots, raisins, and dates.

Put the margarine, sugar, egg, and lemon zest in bowl and beat until smooth and creamy. Sift in the flour, baking powder, baking soda, and salt in a bowl and stir with a fork until well mixed. Add all the fruit to the flour mixture, stir in the reserved fruit liquid, and mix until all is blended. Spoon the batter into the loaf pans. Let the pans stand for 15 minutes, then bake for 45 minutes or until toothpick inserted in the center comes out clean.

Yield: 2 medium loaves.

NO-CHOLESTEROL POPOVERS

We were first introduced to the idea of popovers for breakfast by our friends, Ann and Bill Wilson, innkeepers at The Chester House in Front Royal, Virginia. Their B&B features a majestic home and gardens, and two of the most hospitable hosts anywhere!

These popovers are made without the egg yolks and are guaranteed to "pop-over".

6 egg whites
1 cup skim milk
2 tablespoons margarine, melted
1 cup all-purpose flour
1/4 teaspoon salt
Cooking spray

Beat egg whites at high speed of an electric mixer until foamy. Add milk and margarine; beat at medium speed until well blended. Gradually add flour and salt, beating until smooth.

Pour batter into popover pans (or muffin tins, if you don't have the special pans) coated with cooking spray, filling 3/4 full. Bake at 375° for 50 minutes. Cut a small slit in top of each popover, and cook an additional 5 minutes. Serve immediately.

Yield: 1 dozen popovers.

TOUR OF THE MANOR: THE TOY ROOM

Perhaps the most photogenic of all the guest rooms, the Toy Room is whimsically decorated with a collection of antique quilts and toys. The centerpiece is the antique rocking horse accompanied by a hand-made doll cradle, an old locomotive, and other toys, books and games from childhoods of yesteryear.

The handmade walnut, queen sized canopied bed is extra high, with bed steps...to create the feeling for guests that they are climbing up and being tucked into bed as when they were kids.

Guests in the Toy Room have a french door to take them out to the balcony for a view of the garden, the sunset, and the surrounding countryside. It's a fun and playful room!

SOUTHERN SPOONBREAD

Spoonbread is a dish that dates back to early Colonial days. It's a soufflé-like bread that can be served with the same foods as cornbread or as a replacement for grits at breakfast. I can picture Mary Temperance Booth serving this to her family in this very dining room in the 1820's. The difference is, this recipe retains the delicate flavor and texture of the original Southern spoonbread, without all the fat and calories (which would have been important to the Booth family as they prepared to work on their tobacco plantation ... but we in the 1990's do not require for our more sedentary jobs).

2 cups evaporated skim milk
1 cup water
1 cup white cornmeal
2 tablespoons margarine
1/2 teaspoon salt
2 egg whites
1/2 cup egg substitute
Cooking spray

Combine first 5 ingredients; cook over medium heat until thickened (about 5 minutes), stirring constantly. Remove from heat. Beat egg whites (at room temperature) at medium speed of an electric mixer until stiff. With mixer running, slowly add egg substitute. Gradually stir about 1/3 of hot mixture into egg mixture; add to remaining hot mixture, stirring constantly. Coat 8 (6-ounce) ramekins or a 1 1/2 quart casserole with cooking spray. Divide mixture into ramekins or pour into casserole. Bake in a 350° oven for 20-35 minutes or until a knife inserted in center comes out clean.
Yield: 8 servings.

Compare the nutrients:

Per serving	Tradition version	Light version
Calories	196	119
Fat	9.4 g	2 g
Cholesterol	125 mg	2 mg

SMITH MOUNTAIN VINEYARD

One of Lee's ambitions when we moved to the country was to plant a vineyard and make wine. Having made wine beginning at age 12 (from mulberries), he was enthusiastic about each stage of wine production - from viticulture, to the fermentation, to the "fine tuning" in production that creates superior vintage wine. The wine-grape growing industry in Virginia was just beginning to develop in 1986 when he planted his first vines. He put in two varieties as "test vines", Chardonnay and Gerwurztraminer, planning to expand the vineyard if the site and climate proved to be good for vinifera grapes. Our original idea was to eventually have a full scale commercial vineyard and winery, "Smith Mountain Vineyard", and to produce some of the best wine in Virginia.

As our interest in grapes and wine-making grew, we became acquainted with others throughout the state who were commercially producing wine. We attended several of the state-wide wine festivals, where wineries set up booths for tastings, accompanied by a multitude of other festivities. The idea hit us, "why not introduce the people in our part of the state to this concept and to the delicious Virginia-made wines?".

Together with our friends, Phil and Margaret Hager, we sponsored, organized, and hosted the first "Smith Mountain Lake Wine Festival" in 1989, on the back lawn of The Manor at Taylor's Store. The event was wildly successful - the excellent jazz (provided by Lee's brother, Joe Tucker and some of his fellow musicians), the unique local artisans displaying their wares, the unusual variety of foods to taste, the ten wineries offering samples of their best vintages, the educational seminars throughout the event, and even the "grape stomping trough" - made for an interesting, fun-filled day. We continued to host this special event for two more years, then the popularity of it caused the event to grow beyond our capacity to hold it at The Manor.

The Smith Mountain Lake Wine Festival is now an annual event sponsored by the local Chamber of Commerce, and attended by an ever-increasing crowd.

Meanwhile, back at the vineyard...we have learned alot in the past ten years...grown some nice grapes, made some good wine...but have scaled back our plans from commercial production to just tending the small vineyard and making wine to share with friends. As with aging wine, we have mellowed with time!

CEREALS FOR A HIGH FIBER START

CEREALS FOR A HIGH FIBER START

When our guests arrive in the dining room, hungry and curious, the tantalizing array of buffet items on the huge Empire sideboard portends well for the upcoming feast as well as the day ahead. We always have a fresh, whole grain bread with preserves, honey, and apple butter. There is also a cereal bar ... set up like a "do it yourself sundae" bar ... with two kinds of cereal and a selection of fruits and nuts, so guests can "decorate" their bowl however they like.

Following are some cold and some hot cereal recipes that are interesting even to the guest who eats ready-to-eat boxed cereals everyday at home.

MUESLI I

"Muesli" is a Swiss word that means mush. Back in 1895, Dr. Bircher-Benner invented this combination of fruit and cereal and demonstrated its nutritional value when he successfully treated children with rickets by feeding them Bircher muesli three times a day. You don't have to have a nutritional deficiency to appreciate the healthful benefits of this low-fat, high-fiber way to start your day. The variety of tastes and texture are sure to wake up your taste buds. Feel free to add virtually any fresh fruit or nuts when serving either of the Muesli dishes.

> **1/2 cup soft wheat berries**
> **3 cups water**
> **1/2 cup raisins**
> **1 cup boiling water**
> **2 apples, cored and chopped**
> **1/4 cup lemon juice**
> **1/3 cup uncooked oatmeal**
> **1 banana, sliced**
> **1 cup seedless green grapes**
> **1/4 cup chopped prunes**
> **1/3 cup chopped pecans**
> **1 (8-ounce) carton nonfat plain or lemon yogurt**
> **1/4 cup honey**

Soak wheat berries in 3 cups of water for 8 hours (or overnight); drain. Soak raisins in 1 cup boiled water 15 minutes; drain. Combine chopped apple and lemon juice, tossing well. Combine wheat berries, raisins, apple, lemon juice, oats, and the next 4 ingredients, tossing well. Spoon mixture into bowls. Top with a dollop of yogurt and drizzle with honey.

Yield: 7 Cups or 8 servings.

MUESLI II

This version of muesli can be stored in an airtight container for several breakfasts.

2 1/4 cups rolled oats
1 1/2 cups rolled barley flakes
1 1/2 cups rolled wheat flakes
1 cup raisins
1/2 cup coarsely chopped dried apples
1/2 cup unprocessed oat bran
1/2 cup wheat germ
1/4 cup chopped almonds or hazelnuts
3 tablespoons light brown sugar

In a large bowl, mix all ingredients. Store in an airtight container.
Yield: 8 cups.

PEAR-OATMEAL BAKE

1 (29-ounce) can pear halves, undrained
2 cups milk
2 tablespoons brown sugar
1 tablespoon margarine
1/4 teaspoon salt
1/4 teaspoon cinnamon
1 1/2 cups uncooked oatmeal
1/2 cup chopped pecans
1/4 cup raisins

Drain pears, reserving 1 cup juice. Set aside 2 pears for garnish.
Chop remaining pears; set aside.
Combine 1 cup reserved juice, milk, and next 4 ingredients in a large
saucepan; bring to a boil. Add chopped pears, oats, pecans, and raisins.
Return mixture to a boil. Spoon into lightly greased 2 1/2-quart casserole.
Bake at 350° for 20 minutes. Stir mixture, and bake an additional 5
minutes. Garnish with pear halves.
Yield: 8-10 servings.

EXTRA HIGH FIBER PORRIDGE

Goldilocks would have loved this one!

4 cups water
1/2 cup uncooked oatmeal
1/2 cup uncooked bulgur
1/4 cup uncooked triticale flakes
2 1/2 tablespoons uncooked cream of wheat
2 tablespoons regular grits
1/3 cup raisins
1/4 cup chopped cashews
1/4 cup sunflower kernels, toasted
1/4 cup honey
1 apple, cored, chopped
1 teaspoon ground cinnamon
2 teaspoons margarine
1 cup skim milk

Bring water to boil in a large saucepan; stir in the oats and the next five ingredients. Return to boil; reduce heat, and cook 12-15 minutes, stirring occasionally. You may need to add more water while cooking oats mixture. Stir in raisins and next 6 ingredients. Serve with milk.
Yield: 6-8 servings.

TAYLOR'S STORE LOW-FAT GRANOLA

I began making this granola for Lee shortly after we were married ... to impress him with my domesticity ... and must give credit to Mollie Katzen and "The Enchanted Broccoli Forest" cookbook for the recipe.

Most homemade granola recipes call for a fairly heavy syrup, full of oil and honey, but this recipe is a delicious alternative. It has no oil added, so it involves much less fat and the quick, dry, sauteing give a deep-roasted flavor to the ingredients. The brown sugar melts ever-so-slightly, gently coating each morsel.

On our do-it-yourself-granola-sundae-bar, we have a canister of the granola, a canister of all-bran cereal (for those who are extra-conscious about their fiber intake) and an attractive dish of "toppings" for the cereal. This dish may contain coconut, pecans, almonds, dates, raisins, dried berries, dried bananas, chopped dates, or a trail mix combination of nuts and fruits to sprinkle on top of the cereal.

> **1 cup raw rolled oats**
> **1/3 cup chopped nuts (I like pecans or walnuts)**
> **1/3 cup wheat germ**
> **1/3 cup sesame seeds**
> **1/3 cup sunflower seeds**
> **1/3 cup shredded coconut**
> **1/4 cup brown sugar (packed)**
> **1/4 teaspoon salt**

Use a large, heavy skillet (preferably cast-iron), spray with non-stick cooking spray, and place the oats and the nuts in the skillet, then turn on the heat to medium-low. Stir them constantly for 5 minutes, as they begin to roast. Add wheat germ, sesame seeds, sunflower seeds, and coconut. Keep both the heat and the stirring action constant for 10 more minutes. Sprinkle in brown sugar and salt. Cook for 2-5 more minutes, still stirring. Remove from heat; cool; store in an airtight container.

Yields: 3 Cups. You can double the amounts, but it is recommended that you make smaller batches more frequently instead, for ease in dry-roasting and for greater freshness.

BILL AND GAGA'S "COURTING MUSH"

My grandmother was 70 years old and widowed for 12 years when she fell head over heels in love with a wonderful man. Bill Waugaman, a widower and fellow member of their senior citizens' hand-bell choir, proposed to her over a breakfast he had prepared after one of their Sunday morning bell choir concerts. She didn't hesitate in accepting his offer of marriage (nor in enjoying this special meal). For the 20 years they shared, this "Fried Mush" recipe always evoked romantic memories. It gives a whole new dimension to the word "mushy"!

> 1 cup cornmeal
> 4 cups water, divided
> 1/2 teaspoon salt
> 1/4 cup egg substitute, lightly beaten
> 1/4 cup wheat germ

To cook cornmeal, combine it with 1 cup cold water and mix it into a smooth paste. Bring the remaining 3 cups water to a boil and add salt. When water has come to a boil, slowly add the cornmeal paste, stirring as you add, so that water never stops boiling. Reduce heat to a gentle boil and cook, stirring only enough to keep cereal from sticking. (Too much stirring makes cereal gummy). When liquid is absorbed and grain is tender, remove from heat. Pour cooked cornmeal into a loaf pan that has been lightly oiled. Cover and chill. To serve, unmold, cut into 1/2-inch thick slices, dip into lightly beaten egg substitute, the dredge through the wheat germ and sauté quickly on an oiled skillet or griddle.

Gaga and Bill ate this topped with maple syrup and accompanied by fresh country sausage.

Yield: 4-6 servings.

NORTH AFRICAN BREAKFAST COUSCOUS

An exotic Moroccan import, couscous is an easy-to-cook grain that can be the basis for a meal any time of day. Made from little granules of dried pasta, which is made from semolina (the same grain used to make pasta), couscous is a fat-free version of pasta. Traditional recipes involve a base of couscous topped with a stew of vegetables, meat, and/or fish in a spicy sauce.

This dish can be used either as a first course, or a main course for a breakfast filled with other fresh fruits and whole grain muffins/breads.

2 1/4 cups water
1/4 cup sugar
2 tablespoons orange juice
1 tablespoon margarine
1 1/2 cups uncooked couscous
1/4 cup currants or golden raisins
1 teaspoon cinnamon
Pinch of salt
2 tablespoons finely chopped orange zest
3 navel oranges
10 dates, halved or quartered lengthwise,
    seeds removed
Fresh mint leaves for garnish

Combine water and sugar in a saucepan and bring to a boil. Turn down the heat slightly and boil slowly for 10 minutes, until mixture thickens slightly. Stir in the orange juice and remove from the heat. Stir in the margarine and allow it to melt. Place the couscous in a large bowl. Stir in the currants, cinnamon, salt, and orange zest. Pour into the syrup. Let sit for 20 minutes, stirring from time to time with a wooden spoon. Meanwhile, peel the oranges and cut two of them in half crosswise, then into small sections. Section the third orange, and set aside for garnish. Toss couscous with the chopped oranges. Serve in a small mound, garnished with additional orange and fresh mint.

Yield: 8 servings.

BAKED CHEESE GRITS

Grits are as Southern as magnolia blossoms. I can't understand why enjoyment of them is somewhat controversial, except to think that the name "grits" doesn't have a very appetizing sound to it. I would wager that if you served this dish to unsuspecting diners and didn't tell them what it was until after they tasted it, they'd love it! Broaden your culinary horizons and give it a try!

4 cups water
1 teaspoon salt
1 clove garlic, finely minced
5 tablespoons margarine
1 cup grits
1/2 cup lowfat sharp cheddar cheese
1/2 cup egg substitute
1/3 cup skim milk

Bring water, salt, garlic, and margarine to a boil. Slowly pour in grits, whisk into water, and cook until thick. Mix in cheese. Beat egg substitute and milk. Whisk in. Transfer mixture into casserole or individual ramekins for baking. Bake at 425° for 1 hour.

Yield: 8-10 servings.

BOOKER T. WASHINGTON

The Booker T. Washington National Monument is just 3 miles down the road. It is the birthplace of the famous black educator and author of "Up From Slavery". He was born a slave on the Burroughs plantation, which has now been restored and serves as a living history monument. In addition to farm buildings and livestock, the exhibit has costumed interpreters demonstrating skills and activities that would have been used on early tobacco plantations in this part of the country.

As one might expect, with the proximity of the Burroughs plantation to Taylor's Store, there was a link between the families living there. Anne Burroughs, the daughter of the man who owned Booker T. Washington and his mother, married John Ferguson, living at Taylor's Store. Their daughter, Elizabeth Ferguson Price, subsequently inherited the property and raised her family there until the 1950's, at which time the property passed out of the family for the first time in over 100 years.

PANCAKES, WAFFLES, FRENCH TOAST

LEE'S WHOLE GRAIN PANCAKES

When Lee and I started dating in 1984, one of the things that we both realized we had in common was our love of cooking, especially cooking foods that were deceptively "healthy". Creating low-fat, high-fiber alternatives to the gourmet foods we both loved to eat became a shared interest, and eventually became one of the cornerstones of our B&B project.

This pancake recipe was one that Lee was working on when we met. He subsequently perfected it by weekly practice for Sunday brunch when we were newlyweds.

Any type of whole grain flour may be used ... whole wheat, rye, buckwheat, oat, or any combination thereof. For additional fiber, texture, and flavor you may sprinkle granola, nuts, berries, bananas, or dried fruits on the pancakes after dropping them onto the hot griddle. The pancakes are equally delicious topped with any of the toppings suggested in the "toppings" section or served with butter or butter substitute and real Virginia maple syrup.

> 1 cup "stone-ground" whole grain flour
> 2 tablespoons sugar
> 2 tablespoons baking powder
> 1 teaspoon allspice
> 1/4 teaspoon nutmeg
> 2 egg whites, whipped slightly
> 1 cup skim milk
> 2 tablespoons safflower or canola oil

Combine the first five ingredients. Whip the egg whites slightly, and combine them well with the dry ingredients until the texture resembles cornmeal. Add milk and oil at the same time. Allow the batter to "rise" for at least 20 minutes (this step is very important to a successful pancake!). Spray griddle with cooking spray. If desired, add granola, fruit or nuts to pancakes after they are poured on the griddle.

Yields: 8-10 pancakes, or two large portions.

THE FAMOUS MANOR APPLE PUFFS

If we were to have a "signature" dish, this would be it. We have had more requests from guests for this recipe than any other. It is actually a very old and widely known dish ... having many aliases. It may be called a "German pancake", "Dutch babies", "Clafouti" in Israel, "Yorkshire pudding" in England, and "Apple Puff" in Burnt Chimney.

The chief difference between others and our version is the use of only egg whites to decrease the cholesterol and the preparation of them in individual au gratin style baking dishes. Traditional recipes call for preparation in a large skillet with sloped sides, which you may also do. Most of the traditional recipes suggest baking the pancake first, then topping with fruit or powdered sugar and a sprinkle of lemon. You may also choose to do it that way.

We love the grandiose presentation of the puffs in the individual dishes. Each puffs up with its own personality and those of us in the kitchen each have our own theory about the factors that create the "puffiest" puff ... getting the dishes extra hot ... whipping the eggs in the batter a little extra ... allowing the batter to sit and warm up to room temperature a bit before cooking ... barometric pressure ... attitude of the cook ... the list goes on and on and we chuckle as we develop new theories.

When possible, we use apples from the old trees around the Manor ... from nearby orchards otherwise. In the summer, peaches from local orchards make a scrumptious variation on the theme.

2 pats cannola margarine
1/2 cup egg substitute (2 eggs or 4 whites)
1/2 cup all-purpose flour
1/2 cup skim milk
Dash nutmeg
2 apples, peeled, cored, chopped
Sugar & cinnamon to taste
1/4 cup chopped walnuts
1 tablespoon raisins

Preheat oven to 400°. Mix together egg, flour, milk, and nutmeg with a whisk. Chop apples and toss with cinnamon and sugar. Add nuts and raisins to chopped apples. (You may prepare the apples the night before, but please wait until you are getting ready to cook to prepare the batter). Place a pat of margarine in each of two au gratin size ramekins (9-ounce) and put them into the hot oven. Let the margarine melt and dishes get very hot (at least 5 minutes). Carefully remove the dishes from the oven and ladle 1/2 cup of batter into each. Top with a generous scoop full of the apple, nut, raisin mixture. Immediately return the dishes to the hot oven and bake for 15-20 minutes or until they are puffed up and golden brown. Sprinkle with powdered sugar and serve immediately. We offer Virginia maple syrup for guests to pour on top if they like, but many people find that the fruit and nut mixture adds plenty of sweetness.

Yield: 2 individual ramekin sized servings.

LOWFAT NUT APPLE PANCAKES

This is one of the many wonderful recipes we have received from guests who have stayed with us, appreciated our style of cooking, and sent us their favorite low-fat recipes.

These pancakes use applesauce to substitute for oil to give them the needed texture and moisture ... a trick you can use to modify your own sweet bread and pancake recipes.

1 cup flour (all-purpose or whole wheat)
1/2 teaspoon salt
2 tablespoons baking powder
1 1/2 tablespoons sugar
2 apples, cored, sliced thinly
1 cup skim milk
2 egg whites
1 teaspoon vanilla
2 tablespoons applesauce
1/2 teaspoon apple pie spice
1/2 cup almonds or pecans, chopped

Combine dry ingredients. Combine wet ingredients and add to dry mix. Stir and mix well. Spray griddle, ladle on hot griddle and top with nuts. Cook until bubbles appear, flip.

Sprinkle with powdered sugar and serve with Virginia maple syrup.

Yield: 4-6 large portions.

BANANA WHOLE WHEAT WAFFLES

Waffles have always been my idea of a decadent meal. These combine the fiber of whole wheat, oats, and banana and the calcium of milk and yogurt. Whole eggs are recommended and when the cholesterol in the two eggs are divided into the four servings, each eater only gets the equivalent of 1/2 egg yolk ... well within the American Heart Association guidelines for breakfast.

    1 cup whole wheat flour
    1/2 cup all-purpose flour
    1/2 cup quick-cooking oats
    2 tablespoons sugar
    1/2 teaspoon cinnamon
    1 tablespoon baking powder
    1 ripe banana
    2 eggs
    8 ounces plain non-fat yogurt
    1/2 cup skim milk
    1/4 cup cannola oil

No yogurt? Simply increase milk to 1 cup.
No banana? Try using 1 can (8 1/4-ounces) crushed pineapple, well drained, in place of the banana.

Stir together the flours, oats, sugar, baking powder and cinnamon. In a separate bowl, mash the banana; add remaining ingredients beating lightly until combined. Add banana mixture to dry ingredients; stir until combined. Bake until golden brown, about 90 seconds. Delicious topped with any of the suggested toppings or fruit yogurt.
    Yield: 6-8 waffles or 3-4 servings.

MAPLE WALNUT WAFFLES

Sleeping late on a Saturday morning is such a treat! You can still whip up a batch of these wonderful waffles when you arise because they are easy to prepare using the food processor to save steps. You chop the walnuts at the same time you combine the dry ingredients. As with any food processor recipe, remember you'll get best results if you avoid overprocessing. Use the pulse button and watch the mixture carefully as you process.

2 cups all-purpose flour
1 1/2 teaspoons baking powder
1/2 teaspoon baking soda
1/4 teaspoon salt
1/2 cup walnut halves
1/2 cup egg substitute
1 1/2 cups buttermilk
1/2 cup maple syrup
1/3 cup canola oil

Position knife blade in food processor bowl. Combine the first 5 ingredients in processor bowl; and process for 3 seconds or until the walnuts are coarsely chopped. Add remaining ingredients, and process 5 seconds or until batter is smooth. Bake in a preheated, lightly oiled waffle iron about 5 minutes.

Serve topped with any of the suggested fruit toppings and sprinkled with powdered sugar.

Yield: 8 (8-inch) waffles.

THERE'S A BEAR OUT THERE!

Living in the country, you never know what kind of wildlife you're going to encounter. Guests are forewarned when they go for a walk that there are creatures of all descriptions in this wilderness...hawks, lizards, beavers, fox, turtles, deer, turkey, groundhogs...to name a few. Some very startled guests reported at breakfast that they were sure that they'd seen two huge black bears down at the ponds when they went for their early morning walk. The giant paw-prints on the path had confirmed their sighting. They were quite relieved when I reassured them that our Newfoundland dogs, George and Basil, had been out for a walk that morning ... their resemblance to black bears made for an understandable mistaken identity.

"Every hotel needs a bear." (John Irving, Hotel New Hampshire)...and we have two!

BASIC BLENDER WAFFLES "BEFORE AND AFTER"

Everyone loves waffles! They can be easy and "heart healthy" as demonstrated in this recipe. By substituting egg whites for whole eggs, replacing the oil with applesauce, substituting buttermilk for whole milk, and adding whole wheat flour for flavor and fiber... the result is a lighter and delicious waffle ready to top with fresh fruit and enjoy.

	Calories	Fat (g)	Cholesterol (mg)
BEFORE			
3/4 cup milk	112	6	25
2 eggs	150	10	426
2 tablespoons oil	241	27	0
1 cup flour	455	1	0
1 1/2 teaspoons baking powder	7.5	0	0
1 1/2 teaspoons sugar	24	0	0
1/2 teaspoon salt	0	0	0
TOTAL (whole recipe)	989.5	44	451
4 servings (per serving)	247	11	113
% calories from fat: 40%			
AFTER			
3/4 cup buttermilk	74	1.6	7
4 egg whites	68	0	0
2 tablespoons applesauce	13	0	0
1/2 cup whole wheat flour	204	1	0
1/2 cup white flour	228	0.6	0
1 1/2 teaspoons baking powder	7.5	0	0
1 1/2 teaspoons sugar	24	0	0
TOTAL (whole recipe)	618.5	3.2	7
4 servings (per serving)	155	0.8	2
% calories from fat: 5%			

Lightly oil and preheat waffle iron. In a blender, slightly mix buttermilk, egg whites, and applesauce. Add flour, baking powder, and sugar and blend again briefly. Scrape down the sides of the blender and blend again briefly (overmixing will cause the batter to become too runny).

Ladle 1/4 cup batter onto hot waffle iron and spread evenly to the edge. Bake 4-5 minutes or until steaming stops. Serve topped with any of the suggested toppings.

Yield: 4 (8-inch) waffles.

SWEET POTATO WAFFLES/PANCAKES

Sweet potatoes are a wonderfully versatile vegetable who can disguise themselves as a dessert (as in sweet potato pie), masquerade as a vegetable that even children love (as in yam casserole topped with marshmallows), and can be baked in thin slices with a little salt to create the best-ever home made potato chips. In these waffles/pancakes, the sweet potatoes give a marvelous flavor and texture reminiscent of pumpkin. For that reason, I think of serving them on a crisp fall morning with "Southern Not-Exactly-Fried Apples" or apple-cranberry chutney and a homemade turkey sausage on the side.

3/4 cup peeled, cooked, mashed sweet potatoes (about 1/2 pound raw)
1 1/2 teaspoons cannola oil
1 egg white, slightly beaten
3/4 cup skim milk
1/2 cup whole wheat flour
1 teaspoon baking powder
1/4 teaspoon salt

Preheat waffle iron or large nonstick skillet over medium high heat. Combine cooled sweet potatoes, oil, egg white, and milk in medium size bowl; beat until blended. Add flour, baking powder and salt; stir until smooth.

Coat waffle iron or skillet with cooking oil spray. Ladle batter into waffle iron or skillet by the 1/4 cup Cook until done, flipping pancake over when bubbles pop and dry.

Serve hot with any of the suggested toppings.

Yield: 4 servings.

(Nutritional value per serving: 180 Calories, 6 grams protein, 3 grams fat, 33 grams carbohydrate, 255 milligrams sodium, 4 milligrams cholesterol).

FRENCH TOAST A L'ORANGE

I like to call this "very French" toast ... using croissants and Grand Marnier liqueur adds a richness that more than compensates for the left out egg yolks. The same batter can also be used in the traditional French toast style ... using thick slices of day old French bread. If you do use the French bread, you may pour batter over a layer of bread placed in a baking dish and soak it overnight before grilling it in the morning.

If you don't have Grand Marnier, you may use Triple Sec. Or, if you prefer to cook without the liqueur, you may substitute an extra 1/4 cup of the orange juice and add 1/4 teaspoon of orange extract.

1 1/2 cups egg substitute (or 6 eggs)
2/3 cup orange juice
1/3 cup Grand Marnier liqueur
1/3 cup skim milk
3 tablespoons sugar
1/4 teaspoon vanilla
1/4 teaspoon salt
Finely grated peel of 1 orange
6 croissants (sliced in half as if to make
   a sandwich ... this is easier to do if
   the croissants are frozen first and
   cut while still frozen)

Mix all ingredients together in a bowl and stir well. This may be done the night before and kept covered in the refrigerator. Cut croissants and leave out overnight covered with a cloth so that they will "dry out" a little bit.

In the morning, melt a pat of margarine on griddle over medium-high heat. Dip croissant halves into the batter and cook them until browned (usually 5-8 minutes/side).

We dust the croissants with powdered sugar and garnish with an orange slice and serve with Virginia maple syrup.

Yield: 6 servings.

DECADENT FRENCH TOAST

Credit for this recipe must go to Pat Hardy, executive co-director of the Professional Association of Innkeepers International, who published it in her book, "So You Want to Be An Innkeeper" (see reading list for details about the book). Pat and her partner, Joann Bell, ran the Glenborough Inn in Santa Barbara, California before founding PAII. Pat particularly favored this recipe because it can be put together the night before, enabling the innkeeper to sleep a little later in the morning.

This might be a nice Christmas morning brunch ... allowing the cook to enjoy the morning's festivities and still present a lovely meal for the family.

Once again, we have modified the recipe to remove the egg yolks (you won't even miss them!) and increased the fiber by using "stone-ground" whole wheat bread.

If you find that the caramel topping is too rich for your taste, you can omit it and just layer bread, top with batter, soak overnight and bake the next morning ... equally delicious.

> 2 tablespoons corn syrup
> 1 cup firmly packed brown sugar
> 5 tablespoons cannola margarine
> 16 slices "stone-ground" whole wheat bread
>   or bran bread, crusts removed
> 1 1/2 cups egg substitute (6 eggs)
> 1 1/2 cups skim milk
> 1 teaspoon vanilla extract

Combine corn syrup, brown sugar, and margarine in a small saucepan and heat, stirring, until bubbly. (Don't allow it to continue to boil or you'll have hard caramel candy). Spray a 9x13-inch baking tray with cooking spray and spread the hot caramel syrup evenly on the bottom. Place the bread slices tightly in a layer on top of the syrup. Mix together the egg, milk and vanilla and pour this batter over the bread. Cover the pan and refrigerate overnight. In the morning, preheat the oven to 350°, uncover the French toast tray and bake for 45 minutes or until golden brown.

When you remove the pan from the oven, immediately cover it with a baking tray a little bit larger (we use a cookie sheet) and invert the French toast onto the other tray so that the caramel coating is on the top.

Serve with fresh berries and a sprinkle of powdered sugar. Maple syrup with this dish is overkill, since the caramel topping is quite sweet.

Yield: 6-8 portions, depending upon how you cut the tray.

MANOR MOON PIES

The first time I made this recipe, Agatha Dudley, my dear friend and long time assistant at the B&B said, "those look like moon pies!". This cracked me up ... and since I hadn't officially come up with a name for the dish ...the name "Moon Pie" stuck. It never fails to bring a chuckle at the breakfast table (or a clever guest will ask for an R.C. Cola to go with it!) ... but once they've eaten it, they're hooked!

Pita bread is made without fat, so if you use the non-fat yogurt cheese (recipe on page 154), this is a very lowfat dish.

8 whole wheat pita breads
1/2 cup lowfat yogurt cheese or Neufchatel cheese
2 1/2 tablespoons strawberry preserves (or you can use raspberry or peach if you prefer)
2 cups egg substitute (equal to 8 eggs)
1 cup skim milk
2 teaspoons vanilla
2 tablespoons sugar
2 cups fresh strawberries, sliced and lightly sugared

Cut each pita bread in half to make two "pockets". Combine the cheese and preserves in food processor until well blended. Mix together in a medium bowl, the egg substitute, milk, vanilla, and sugar and stir well.

Carefully open one pita pocket and spread 1 tablespoon of the fruited cheese over the inside. Repeat this with each of the halves. Preheat griddle to 350° (medium heat), spray with cooking spray or spread a small amount of margarine on griddle to prevent sticking. Carefully dip each pita pocket in the egg/milk batter and place it on the griddle. Cook until browned, flip and cook until browned on the reverse side.

To serve, layer two of the crescent shaped pitas just overlapping each other. Top with fresh strawberries and a sprinkle of powdered sugar.

Yield: 8 servings.

ANGLER'S PARADISE

Fishermen find their haven in the six ponds on the estate. The eight acres of water are stocked with largemouth bass, crappie, and blue gill, exclusively for the fishing challenges of B&B guests. Both fly-fishing and bait-casting, from shore, dock, or from the canoe, may be productive and is sure to be fun for those who like to fish. Largemouth bass over eight pounds have been caught (and most guests return them to the pond for the next guest to catch!).

Non-fishing companions can relax in the gazebo, swim in the largest pond, take the canoe out for a paddle, or hike the trails surrounding this waterfront paradise.

COUNTRY CORNCAKES

The Blue Ridge Parkway is a scenic byway that winds along atop the Blue Ridge Mountains from Front Royal, Virginia all the way down to the Great Smokies in North Carolina and Tennessee. We are very fortunate that this beautiful road passes right through Roanoke, and only 20 miles from The Manor. Its proximity makes it so easy for Lee and I to go for a nice drive and hike on a crisp fall day. Mabry Mill is an old gristmill, still in operation, just a 45 minute drive south on the Parkway. It is understandably said to be the "most photographed" place along that extremely photogenic drive. Not only is Mabry Mill picturesque, but it also has a little cafe which serves wonderful griddle cakes using the grain ground at the mill. My idea of a perfect fall day - an early hike off the Parkway followed by a big platter of Mabry Mill Corncakes!

This version of corncakes has the additional benefit of fresh corn and no cholesterol.

1 cup fresh corn cut from the cob (about 2 ears)
1/2 cup yellow cornmeal
1 cup boiling water
2 teaspoons honey
1/4 teaspoon salt
2 egg whites
Cooking spray

Cook corn, covered, in boiling water 8-10 minutes, or until tender; drain and set aside to cool. Combine corn and next 4 ingredients in a medium bowl; stir well. Beat egg whites at high speed of an electric mixer until stiff peaks form. (Do not overbeat.) Fold egg whites into corn mixture.

Preheat griddle to medium-high. Spray with cooking spray. Pour 1/4 cup batter onto hot griddle. Cook 3 minutes on each side or until brown. Great served with Virginia maple syrup and lean, grilled ham sprinkled with a little clove!

Yield: 12 (3 1/2-inch) corncakes.

POTATO PANCAKES - LUSCIOUS LATKES

Our first introduction to latkes was at a Hanukkah dinner at our friends, Lew and Wendy Singer's home. They explained to us that this Hanukkah specialty is a tradition because the oil that it is cooked in relates to the Hanukkah story. A little over 2,000 years ago, the Jews in Israel were in danger of being forced to worship Greek gods, but they managed to drive the invading army out of Jerusalem. When they wanted to rekindle the holy temple's light, however, they could find only enough oil to last one day. Miraculously, the oil lasted eight days. This is why Hanukkah is called the Festival of Lights, and is celebrated for eight days with candles. Besides our enjoyment in learning about and celebrating this holiday with our friends, we learned to love these potato pancakes!

They make a marvelous breakfast served with applesauce and a dollop of sour cream (plain yogurt is a good substitute) and a slice of clove-grilled turkey ham.

4 large potatoes, scrubbed, but not peeled
1 medium onion
1 large egg (or 1/4 cup egg substitute)
1 tablespoon wheat germ
1 teaspoon salt
1/4 teaspoon ground white pepper
2 tablespoons whole wheat flour
1 tablespoon safflower oil
Non stick pan spray
1/4 cup lemon juice in 2 quarts of water

After scrubbing potatoes, finely shred them (a food processor with a grating disc makes this job ever so much easier). Submerge the potato shreds in the lemon water to prevent their discoloration. Stir well, drain, and pat them dry in a colander using paper towels to press out as much liquid as possible.

Grate or finely mince the onion and combine it in a large bowl with the potato shreds. Add egg, wheat germ, salt, pepper, and flour and mix to combine well.

Preheat oven to 400°. Spray a skillet or griddle with nonstick cooking spray and add 1/2 teaspoon oil. Spoon in about 2 tablespoons of batter for each pancake and spread into a thin circle (don't worry if holes appear). Don't make the cakes much larger than 3-inches or they'll be too difficult to handle. Cook 2-3 pancakes at a time, turning once, until golden on both sides. Add a little more oil or re-spray pan between cooking batches, if needed. As pancakes are cooked, lift out and place in a single layer on a baking sheet.

(Cakes can be prepared up to 12 hours ahead of time up to this point, covered and refrigerated until ready to bake. They can also be frozen on the baking sheet, and when frozen transferred to a plastic bag. If frozen, thaw briefly before baking.) When all the cakes are made, put the baking sheet into the oven, uncovered, until crisp and brown, 8-10 minutes.

Yield: 14-16 latkes, or 4 generous servings.

TO TOP IT OFF...

Each of the preceding recipes for pancakes, waffles, and French toast are excellent as they are, just served with maple syrup, molasses (Lee's favorite), or butter/margarine and a sprinkling of powdered sugar. However, for that extra special touch, we like to add a topping to jazz up the presentation and to lend another taste/texture to the dish.

Following are a few of the infinite ideas for topping your dishes. Use these suggestions as a starting point to expand into your own creativity. I like to think of this section as a "mix and match" format ... like those clever children's books that are cut into sections with different heads, arms, bodies, and legs that you can combine into an endless variety of creatures. Any of the recipes in this chapter are great with any of these toppings ... try them all! Your imagination is the only limit!

BLUEBERRY AMARETTO SAUCE

1/2 cup water
1 tablespoon Amaretto (or 1 teaspoon almond extract,
**   if you prefer not to use liqueur)**
2 teaspoons cornstarch
3/4 cup fresh blueberries (or frozen, if fresh aren't
**   available ... thaw and drain well)**
2 teaspoons lemon juice

Combine water, Amaretto, and cornstarch in a small non-aluminum saucepan; stir well. Add blueberries, cook over medium heat 5 minutes or until thickened, stirring constantly. Remove from heat; stir in lemon juice.

This sauce is superb on the crepes filled with almond cream filling. It is also quite nice drizzled on a plate, topped with a waffle, then further topped with fresh peaches.

Yield: 1 cup.

RASPBERRY AND/OR PEACH MELBA SAUCE

2 cups fresh or frozen raspberries
2 tablespoons honey
1/2 teaspoon vanilla
2 teaspoons arrowroot or cornstarch
1/4 cup water
2 cups fresh peaches, peeled, sliced,
    and lightly sugared

In a small saucepan, combine raspberries, honey, and vanilla. Stir over low heat until just below boiling. Mix starch and water, and add to raspberry mixture. Cook over low heat until thickened, about 5 minutes. This results in a jam-like consistency. Or, if you prefer, the raspberries can be strained through a sieve.

This sauce is yummy all by itself on top of any of the recipes. For the "Peach Melba" variation, ladle 1/4 cup of the Raspberry Sauce on the plate, top with whichever pancake, waffle, French toast or crepe you choose. Then, pile loads of the fresh, sugared peaches on top of it all and dash a bit of powdered sugar on the tip top. A garnish of a fresh raspberry and mint leaves is a lovely addition!

ANY BERRY SAUCE

One of the beauties of living in the country is that summer provides a parade of fresh berries that we can integrate into our breakfasts. In May the local strawberry fields have their "U-Pick-Em" signs up and it's wonderful fun to spend the day filling baskets (as well as your tummy) with the ripe red berries. Raspberries and blueberries appear in the Roanoke Farmer's Market beginning in June. And by the end of June, the blackberry bushes all over our estate are full of fruit (it's fun to pick as long as you're wearing a long sleeved shirt!).
This sauce is delicious on top of any of the recipes.

2/3 cup sugar
2 tablespoons cornstarch
Dash cinnamon, dash nutmeg
1 cup water
2 cups blueberries, strawberries, raspberries,
    blackberries, or any combination thereof
2 teaspoons lemon juice

Combine first four ingredients in saucepan. Gradually add water. Cook over medium heat stirring constantly. Bring to a boil. Boil one minute; stir in berries, cook one minute. Remove from heat, add lemon juice. Cool slightly and serve over pancakes, waffles or crepes.

APPLE-CRANBERRY CHUTNEY

I think this particular topping is at its best with the "Sweet Potato Pancakes/Waffles". It also makes a nice accompaniment to Pumpkin Muffins or Pumpkin Soufflé (or even Thanksgiving dinner!).

2 cups peeled, chopped apples
1 cup cranberries
1/4 cup golden raisins
2 tablespoons brown sugar
1 tablespoon grated orange rind
2 tablespoons cider vinegar
1/4 teaspoon ground cloves
1/4 teaspoon ground nutmeg
1/4 teaspoon ground cinnamon

Combine all ingredients in a non-aluminum saucepan. Place over high heat. Bring to a boil; stir constantly. Reduce heat and simmer, uncovered, 15 minutes or until apples are tender. Remove from heat and let cool. Position knife blade in food processor bowl; add cranberry mixture. Top with cover and process, pulsing 1-2 times, until combined.

Serve warm, room temperature, or chilled.

Yield: 2 cups.

ANGLER'S PARADISE

Fishermen find their haven in the six ponds on the estate. The eight acres of water are stocked with largemouth bass, crappie, and blue gill, exclusively for the fishing challenges of B&B guests. Both fly-fishing and bait-casting, from shore, dock, or from the canoe, may be productive and is sure to be fun for those who like to fish. Largemouth bass over eight pounds have been caught (and most guests return them to the pond for the next guest to catch!).

Non-fishing companions can relax in the gazebo, swim in the largest pond, take the canoe out for a paddle, or hike the trails surrounding this waterfront paradise.

YOGURT TOPPINGS

One of my life's greatest adventures was the opportunity I had to live in Greece and attend a special arts school there as a part of my college education. One of my favorite memories of that time was leaving my little flat over the "Souvlaki" stand and making my way to class through the hustle and bustle of downtown Athens (the smell of diesel from buses still evokes a nostalgia). Along the way, at Omonia Square, was a little "dairy shop" with big trays of freshly made yogurt. I loved to stop there and order a generous slab of the yogurt drizzled with honey, to be eaten with a hard roll and a very strong cup of Turkish coffee. Ahhh ... culinary memories evoke so many pleasurable feelings! So, I come by my love of yogurt ... and enjoy using that in cooking as well as just snacking.

Yogurt makes a very easy, very healthful topping, combined with fruit or preserves. We like to use the non-fat plain yogurt and "doctor" it up ourselves. For all of these recipes, you can either stir or food process the ingredients into the plain yogurt. Then fold in the preserves. There is no limit to the variations on this theme ... but here are a few ideas for starters:

* 1 cup yogurt, 2 tablespoons honey, 1 teaspoon lemon juice, 1/4 teaspoon lemon zest to create a lemon yogurt. This can be combined with sour cherry preserves, raspberry preserves, or blackberry jam.

* 1 cup yogurt, 2 tablespoons honey, 1/4 teaspoon vanilla to make vanilla yogurt. Fold in strawberry, raspberry, or peach preserves.

* 1 cup yogurt, 2 tablespoons honey, 1 tablespoon orange juice concentrate (thawed) to create orange yogurt. Add fresh blueberries, raspberries, or canned, drained mandarin oranges.

* 1 cup yogurt, 2 tablespoons honey, 2 canned peach halves (this one does best in food processor) to create peach yogurt. Fold in raspberry preserves.

ORANGE SAUCE

Try this one with the "French Toast A L'orange" or with crepes filled with an orange cream filling.

>   2 tablespoons sugar
>   1 tablespoon cornstarch
>   3/4 cup water
>   2 tablespoons orange juice concentrate (thawed)
>   1 11-ounce can mandarin oranges, drained
>   1 tablespoon chopped walnuts

Combine sugar and cornstarch in saucepan. Stir in water and orange juice concentrate. Cook until thick and bubbly. Reduce heat and cook 2 minutes. Add mandarin oranges and walnuts. Serve warm.

EASY BLENDER STRAWBERRY SAUCE

If you want to make a berry sauce in the dead of winter ... this recipe works fine with frozen berries. Simply thaw and drain the berries in a colander before proceeding with the recipe.

>   2 cups fresh (or frozen) strawberries
>   1 tablespoon sugar
>   1 tablespoon vanilla

Put all ingredients in the blender or food processor and process until smooth. Heat through and serve warm.

This is particularly good with the blintzes.

THE MANY MANIFESTATIONS OF MAGNIFICENT CREPES

THE MANY MANIFESTATIONS OF MAGNIFICENT CREPES

Imagine a recipe that you can make ahead and store in your freezer, to be retrieved at a moment's notice and converted into innumerable elegant and delicious gourmet creations for breakfast, brunch, a hearty dinner, or dessert. Crepes are just that ... these delicate and versatile little French pancakes are an innkeeper's dream come true!

Following are a basic crepe recipe and several suggestions for ways to prepare and present them. These are just a few of the infinite possibilities for crepe creativity. Let your imagination go wild in developing your own ideas from here!

WHOLE WHEAT CREPES

1/2 cup white flour
1/2 cup whole wheat flour
1 cup skim milk
1/2 cup egg substitute (or 2 eggs or 4 egg whites)
1 tablespoon safflower oil

Combine all 5 ingredients in the container of an electric blender; process for 10 seconds. Scrape down the sides of the blender container with a rubber spatula; process 10 seconds or until smooth. Refrigerate batter for 1 hour (this is an important step ... enabling the flour particles to swell and soften to create light and delicate crepes ... don't be in a hurry).

Spray a 6-inch crepe pan or small nonstick skillet and place it over medium heat until just hot, not smoking. Pour 2 tablespoons batter into pan and quickly tilt the pan in all directions so that the batter covers the pan in a thin film. Cook for about 30 seconds, then lift the edge of the crepe to test for doneness. The crepe is ready for flipping when it can be shaken loose from the pan. Flip and cook 30 seconds on the other side. When the crepe is done, place it on a plate to cool. Stack the crepes between layers of waxed paper to prevent sticking.

Yield: 18-24 (6-inch) crepes (serves 6-8 people).

ELEGANT NUT CREAM CREPES

So delicious, your guests won't believe that they're actually low fat!

1/4 cup nuts (almonds, pecans, walnuts, hazelnuts ... choose one)
1 cup lowfat cottage cheese
1 teaspoon vanilla extract (if using almonds, use almond extract; hazelnuts with hazelnut extract; maple extract is good with pecans or walnuts)
2 tablespoons sugar

In bowl of food processor, place nuts and pulse for a few seconds until nuts are coarsely chopped. Remove them from the processor bowl and put them aside momentarily. Put cottage cheese, extract, and sugar together into processor bowl and process thoroughly until the cottage cheese is creamy and smooth (be certain to process until the texture resembles whipped cream, with none of the grainy texture of the cottage cheese still visible). Fold in the chopped nuts.

Spoon about 2 tablespoons of the cream filling along one edge of unbrowned side of a crepe ... and roll crepe up, placing rolled side down on plate to hold it closed. Two nut cream filled crepes topped with any of the suggested fruit toppings (from Part 2 of this chapter) make an ample serving.

Alternatively, you may prepare a fruit filling using the fruit topping recipes ... and top with a dollop of the nut cream. Use your own creativity!

SAVORY GARDEN CREPES

1 cup chicken broth
3 cups broccoli, broken into smallest flowerettes
1 cup thinly sliced carrots
2/3 cup sliced fresh mushrooms
2 tablespoons thinly sliced green onions
2 tablespoons all-bran cereal

Dijon Sauce:

1 (8-ounce) carton plain non-fat yogurt
1 tablespoon Dijon mustard
1/2 teaspoon prepared horseradish

Heat chicken broth in a heavy skillet; add broccoli and carrots, and cook, uncovered, 5 minutes. Add mushrooms and green onions; cook 2 minutes or until vegetables are crisp-tender and liquid is evaporated. Stir in cereal.

Spoon vegetable mixture (using slotted spoon to further drain juice from vegetables) by 1/2 cup portions onto the edge of unbrowned side of crepes. Roll crepe and place fold side down on the plate to keep it rolled.

To make the Dijon Sauce, simply combine all ingredients and mix well. Yield: 1 cup (enough for 8 servings). Two vegetable filled crepes topped with 2 tablespoons of the Dijon Sauce makes a hearty serving.

HOW DID THE CHRISTMAS COTTAGE GET IT'S NAME?

Families and groups travelling together find their own private paradise at our little Christmas Cottage. It is a separate home with three bedrooms, two baths, a fully equipped kitchen, a den with a fireplace, and two nice decks for enjoying the secluded woods in which it is located. Sitting on the hillside overlooking the ponds, the Cottage has also been a favorite spot for honeymooners who want total privacy for their getaway. In contrast to the elegant antiques and oriental rugs in The Manor, the Cottage is appointed with very comfortable modern furnishings, more appropriate to a little cabin in the woods.

We often get asked why we call it the "Christmas Cottage". There are several answers to this question. First of all, we bought the cottage and the acreage it is on the second Christmas we lived here...so it was like a Christmas gift to us. Secondly, we proceeded to plant acres of white pines on the property...future Christmas trees. Another "Christmas" feature of the Cottage is that I leave my wonderful Santa Claus collection out on display there all year round. The teasing answer is (of course), "it's Christmas...no room in the inn"!

APRICOT CREPES WITH ORANGE CRUNCH TOPPING

2 (16-ounce) cans apricot halves in light syrup, drained
1/4 cup frozen orange juice concentrate, thawed, undiluted
1 tablespoon cornstarch
1/8 teaspoon almond extract
1 recipe of crepes (12 crepes)
1 tablespoon frozen orange juice concentrate, thawed
1/2 cup lowfat sour cream (or substitute on page 155)
1/8 teaspoon ground mace
4 vanilla wafers, coarsely crushed

Drain apricot halves, reserving 1/2 cup liquid. Cut apricots in quarters, and set aside.

Combine reserved apricot liquid and 1/4 cup orange juice concentrate; stir well. Combine 2 tablespoons of this mixture and cornstarch in a small non-aluminum saucepan; gradually add remaining orange juice mixture, stirring well. Place over medium-high heat; bring to a boil. Cook 1 minute, stirring constantly. Remove from heat. Stir in apricots and almond extract. Place mixture in bowl and cover and chill for 1 hour.

Spoon 2 tablespoons apricot mixture in center of crepe. Fold crepe in half, then in half again to form a triangle. Repeat procedure with remaining crepes and apricot mixture. Place 2 crepes on each serving plate and garnish with mint sprigs.

Combine sour cream, remaining 1 tablespoon orange juice concentrate, and mace in a small bowl; stir in cookie crumbs. Serve over crepes.

Yield: 12 crepes, 6 servings (or 4 large portions).

SPINACH CREPE QUICHES

1 (10-ounce) package frozen chopped spinach
1 cup (4 ounces) shredded low fat Swiss cheese
1 cup (4 ounces) shredded skim mozzarella cheese
2 tablespoons all-purpose flour
1 1/3 cups skim milk
1 cup egg substitute
1/4 cup diced onion
1/4 teaspoon salt
1/8 teaspoon pepper
1/4 teaspoon dried whole thyme
1/4 teaspoon dried whole rosemary, crushed
1/8 teaspoon hot sauce

Cook spinach according to package directions, omitting salt. Drain well, and press spinach between paper towels until barely moist. Set aside.

Combine cheeses and flour; toss well and set aside. Combine milk and next 7 ingredients in a mixing bowl, stirring well. Stir in spinach and cheese mixture, mixing well.

Spray six (6 ounce) custard cups with cooking spray. Line each cup with a crepe. Spoon spinach mixture into each crepe-lined custard cup. Place cups on a cookie sheet; bake at 325° for 45 minutes or until set. (Place a piece of foil over quiches after baking 15 minutes to prevent edges from getting too brown.)

Yield: 6 servings.

TOUR OF THE MANOR: THE COLONIAL ROOM

With its queen sized canopied bed and balcony overlooking the garden and estate, the Colonial Room is a very popular guest room. The walnut bed was hand made for us by an elderly gentleman living in the mountains of North Carolina...ordered through an artists' coop on the Blue Ridge Parkway. The french doors leading to the balcony beckon guests to relax and watch the sunset or take a cup of tea outside on a starry night.

PORK AND FRUIT CREPES

1/2 cup apple juice
1/2 cup dry red wine
1 tablespoon cornstarch
1/4 teaspoon minced fresh thyme
Cooking spray
1 pound lean ground pork
3/4 teaspoon fennel seeds, crushed
1/2 teaspoon salt
1 clove garlic, minced
3 cups coarsely chopped, unpeeled apples (about 2)
10 small fresh figs, quartered (may use dried)
1 crepe recipe

Combine the first 4 ingredients in a medium non-aluminum saucepan; stir until cornstarch dissolves. Bring to a boil; cook over high heat 1 minute, stirring constantly. Set aside.

Coat a large nonstick skillet with cooking spray; place over medium heat until hot. Add pork and next 4 ingredients; cook 4 minutes, stirring to crumble. Add apples; cook an additional 2 minutes or until pork is browned, stirring frequently. Drain pork mixture in a colander, and pat dry with paper towels. Combine pork, wine mixture, and quartered figs, stirring well.

Spoon 1/2 cup pork mixture down center of each crepe; roll up, and place, seam side down, in a 13x9x2-inch baking dish. Cover and bake at 350° for 15 minutes. Top with fresh thyme sprigs for garnish. Serve warm.

Yield: 12 crepes (may be 12 or 6 hearty servings).

OUR OWN ECO-HABITAT: THE PONDS

The history of the ponds on the estate is an interesting slice of eco-history. There are six ponds now running down through a steeply wooded valley in the middle of the estate. The top pond was originally the only pond. In the old days, this was the local "ice pond". Before the spring thaw, huge blocks of ice were cut from the pond and hauled up to the ice house (located on the hillside next to the Manor). The ice was sold at Taylor's Store, and elderly residents recall that it usually lasted until late summer. This is an indication that the weather has become more temperate in recent years...as the pond has only frozen over solidly twice in the ten years we've lived here.

The other five ponds were created in the early 1940's. After World War II, there were men and machinery (and government subsidies) for large farm projects. Since the ponds are all spring-fed, we surmised that they were created to reclaim swampy land as well as to create a water source for agricultural use.

When we arrived in 1986, they had been very poorly maintained...shorelines invisible for overgrowth, pond surfaces overgrown with weeds, dams failing. We proceeded to drain the ponds, re-build dams, re-plant grass and trees, create paths, build swimming and fishing docks, and create the recreational paradise that now exists.

In addition to the resident gaggle of geese, the ponds have become home to transient flocks of wild ducks and geese. They support their own eco-system of turtles, birds, fish, and mammals. The local deer use them for a watering hole (protected from hunters). Our "weed control" program in the ponds consists of special carp that we introduced to the ponds (vegetarians that weigh up to 40 lbs. and eat their weight in weeds every day!).

We are honored to be the stewards for this private "Walden"!

EGGS: TO EAT OR NOT TO EAT

EGGS - TO EAT OR NOT TO EAT?

In recent nutrition history, perhaps no single food has caused as much controversy as the simple egg. Researchers, physicians, dieticians, and consumers can't seem to agree on whether the nutritional benefits of eggs outweigh their high cholesterol count, in the overall scheme of health. Let me briefly present a few of the key arguments ... and leave it up to you to decide whether whole eggs are for you or not.

In defense of the egg, it is truly one of Nature's most perfect foods, in terms of its biological structure. The protein found in eggs is of the highest quality for human nutrition. A serving of 2 eggs provides about 14 grams of this protein, plus 12 grams of fat, 1 gram of carbohydrate, and at least 13 minerals and 13 vitamins - all for only 160 calories. So, with a food this wholesome, what is the controversy?

Eggs are also the most concentrated source of cholesterol in the American diet, the yolk of one egg containing between 250-275 milligrams of cholesterol. If you follow the dietary guidelines of the American Heart Association and other public health policy organizations, their recommendations are for a maximum intake of 300 milligrams of cholesterol per day. Eating one egg a day doesn't leave much room for any other foods containing cholesterol.

Here's where the controversy escalates. Several studies have demonstrated no significant effect on blood cholesterol from regular egg intake. On the other side, some carefully controlled studies have shown that as egg yolk was added to diets of subjects, blood cholesterol levels did rise. Some egg enthusiasts argue that egg yolks also contain lethicin, which is said to emulsify cholesterol and dislodge it from blood vessels. Egg antagonists site studies that show that even if total cholesterol level is not increased by increasing egg yolk consumption, there is an increase in a type of cholesterol-carrying lipoprotein that is even more damaging to blood vessels than the dreaded LDL. Egg supporters contend that it is saturated fats that are the worst offenders in raising blood cholesterol levels, and eggs are not high in saturated fats ... and this is where the debaters shake hands ... both agreeing that saturated fats are a mutual enemy.

So, should you eat eggs or not? The decision is yours to make, based on the recommendations of your physician or dietician and the depth of your concern about and interest in your blood cholesterol/blood fat profile. We are not recommending one point of view or the other.

However, the recipes in this section all use egg whites and egg substitute, to offer those of you who do wish to limit egg yolks some creative and delicious alternatives to using whole eggs. I felt that those who are egg-lovers have no limit to luscious egg recipes in any cookbook they may find, and in most cases these recipes can be made using whole eggs for those who prefer them. So, hopefully there will be something for both schools of thought on the egg issue in this section.

SUBSTITUTES FOR WHOLE EGGS

"People who are cutting down on their cholesterol intake by eliminating eggs ... don't get the yolk!" (or "the yolk's on you!")

There are several alternatives for adapting recipes for egg dishes to leave out the egg yolk. You can use two egg whites for each whole egg called for in the recipe, which works well in pancake and muffin recipes. However, using only egg whites in quiches, omelets, French toast, or frittatas results in a pale, rather unappetizing product. For recipes like these, an egg substitute is best.

There are several varieties of commercial egg substitutes available. In addition to egg whites, most contain oil, coloring, sodium, and preservatives to help them taste and perform like whole eggs. While egg substitutes can decrease calorie, fat, and cholesterol, they can increase the cost to make a recipe.

An alternative is to make your own egg substitute:

6 egg whites
1/4 cup instant nonfat dry milk powder
2 tablespoons water
1 1/2 teaspoons vegetable oil
1/4 teaspoon ground turmeric

Combine all ingredients in container of an electric blender or food processor. Process 30 seconds. Refrigerate up to 1 week or freeze in an airtight container up to 1 month.

Yield: 3/4 cup (each serving of 1/4 cup is one egg equivalent and contains: 90 calories, 10.6 gram protein, 2.4 gram fat, 6 gram carbohydrate, 2 milligram cholesterol, 162 milligram sodium, and 130 milligram calcium).

VIRGINIA SMITHFIELD HAM SAUSAGE SOUFFLÉ

We were most flattered to have been featured in Southern Living magazine in May, 1993, as one of their six favorite B&B's. This was one of the recipes from our inn that they featured in that article. The Virginia Smithfield Ham sausage is a specialty item that is only available in certain stores, and only in Virginia. An excellent substitute is one of the homemade lowfat sausages in the "Meat" chapter of this cookbook.

1 pound Virginia ham sausage (or turkey sausage)
4 green onions, chopped
1-2 cloves garlic, minced
2 cups egg substitute
1 cup skim milk
1/4 teaspoon salt
1/4 teaspoon ground red pepper
3/4 teaspoon dry mustard
6 slices whole wheat bread, cubed

Cook first 3 ingredients in a large skillet until sausage is browned, stirring until sausage crumbles; drain. Rinse with hot water; drain well, and press between layers of paper towels. Set aside. Combine egg substitute and next 4 ingredients in a large bowl; stir in sausage mixture and bread cubes. Spoon into 10 (6-ounce) ramekins or custard cups coated with cooking spray; cover and chill for 8 hours (or overnight). Remove from refrigerator 30 minutes before baking. Bake, uncovered, at 350° for 30 minutes or until set. Serve immediately.
Yield: 10 servings.

FABULOUS FRITTATAS

A frittata is an Italian omelet made with the filling in the eggs and served flat. There is no limit to the toppings you can use to make this tasty dish. The procedure for cooking a frittata is the same for each rendition.

Italian cookbooks suggest that when the eggs are soft set on top and the bottom is lightly browned, place a serving-size plate or flat cookie sheet over the pan and reverse the frittata onto it. Tap the skillet firmly to release the eggs. Then slide the frittata back into the skillet to brown the second side. The resulting dish is then slid onto a serving platter.

Another method is to use a skillet with an oven-proof handle, cook the first side over medium-low heat until the eggs are almost set (about 10 minutes). Then remove the skillet from the stove top and place it under a preheated broiler until completely set (3-5 minutes). You may then either slide it from the skillet onto serving platter or cut into wedges and serve on individual plates.

Here are a few interpretations of the frittata ... use your imagination to go from here!

VEGETABLE FRITTATA

1 cup egg substitute
1 tablespoon skim milk
1/4 teaspoon dried oregano
1/8 teaspoon salt
1/8 teaspoon pepper
Olive oil flavored cooking spray
1/8 teaspoon minced fresh garlic
1/4 cup finely chopped onion
1/4 cup chopped sweet red pepper
1/4 cup chopped broccoli flowerettes
1/4 cup alfalfa sprouts
2 tablespoons sliced fresh mushrooms
2 ounces (1/2 cup) shredded reduced fat Swiss cheese

Combine first 5 ingredients in a medium bowl; beat well. Coat a small non-stick oven-proof skillet with cooking spray; add garlic, onion, red pepper and broccoli, and sauté until tender. Remove vegetables from skillet, and add egg mixture. Reduce heat to low; cover and cook 8-10 minutes or until set. Top with alfalfa sprouts, sauteed vegetables, and mushrooms. Sprinkle evenly with cheese. Remove from stove and finish under broiler for about 1 minute, just to melt cheese. Serve immediately.

Yield: 4 servings.

ITALIAN FARMER'S FRITTATA

1 cup egg substitute
1 tablespoon skim milk
1/4 teaspoon salt
1/8 teaspoon pepper
1/4 teaspoon Italian seasoning
1/2 teaspoon olive oil
1/2 cup chopped onion
2 tablespoons chopped green pepper
2 cloves garlic, minced
4 small red potatoes, diced (unpeeled is best)
1 tablespoon grated Parmesan cheese
1/2 cup shredded lowfat mozzarella cheese
Optional marinara sauce for accompaniment

Combine the first 5 ingredients in a bowl and beat well. Heat the olive oil in a small non-stick oven proof skillet. Add onion, green pepper, and garlic; sauté until crisp-tender. Add potatoes; cook 5-8 minutes, stirring often, until potatoes begin to brown. Reduce heat to medium-low and pour egg mixture over vegetables in the skillet, then sprinkle with Parmesan cheese and mozzarella. Cover and cook 8-10 minutes until just set. Finish under broiler to lightly brown the top (about 1 minute). Cut into 4 wedges. Serve with a condiment dish of warmed marinara sauce for guests to add if they like.

Yield: 4 servings.

FIESTA TOSTADO

My love for Mexican food knows no bounds! When Lee and I went to Texas to visit relatives several years ago, he was astonished that we ate Mexican dishes for breakfast, lunch, and dinner. (He did get a "break" one night and ate some of the world's best spicy Texas barbecue!) My father, raised in the Rio Grande Valley of Texas, was fond of joking that a daily dose of hot chilies "kept your blood flowing". Remedial qualities aside, spicy foods are an interesting way to wake up your taste buds and add variety to your morning meal!

4 (8 1/2-inch) flour tortillas
1/2 cup (2 ounces) shredded reduced fat cheddar cheese
1 (4-ounce) can chopped green chilies, drained
1/4 cup sliced green onions
1/2 cup salsa or picante sauce
1 cup egg substitute
1/3 cup skim milk
1/2 teaspoon chili powder
1/4 teaspoon cracked black pepper
6 tomato slices
2 tablespoons plain nonfat yogurt
Sprigs of fresh cilantro

Coat a 12-inch quiche dish with cooking spray; layer tortillas in dish. Sprinkle cheese, chilies, and green onions over tortillas; dollop with salsa or picante sauce. Combine egg substitute and next 3 ingredients; pour into quiche dish. Bake at 350° for 30-35 minutes. Remove from oven, and arrange tomato slices around edge of quiche; top each tomato slice with 1 teaspoon yogurt and a sprig of cilantro. Cut into wedges.
    Yield: 6 servings.

EGGS BENEDICT

This breakfast and brunch classic traditionally packs a two-fold cholesterol punch ... both in the poached eggs and in the yolk-rich Hollandaise Sauce that tops it off. Try this alternative recipe, and compare the cholesterol savings.

4 slices lean Canadian bacon
1 cup egg substitute
2 whole wheat English muffins, split & toasted
Mock Hollandaise Sauce
Paprika and parsley for garnish

Coat a large non-stick skillet with cooking spray; place over medium heat until hot. Add Canadian bacon, and cook until thoroughly heated, turning once. Remove from heat; keep warm.

Place 1/4 cup egg substitute in each of 4 (6-ounce) custard cups coated with cooking spray. Cover loosely with wax paper; microwave at HIGH 1 1/2 - 2 1/2 minutes, giving cups a half-turn after 45 seconds. Let stand 2 minutes.

Place 1 bacon slice on each muffin half; top each with cooked egg substitute and 3 tablespoons Mock Hollandaise Sauce. Sprinkle with paprika. Garnish with parsley.

Yield: 4 servings (or 2 large portions).

MOCK HOLLANDAISE SAUCE

1/2 cup plain nonfat yogurt
1/4 cup reduced fat mayonnaise
2 teaspoons lemon juice
1/8 ground red pepper
(Optional 1/4 teaspoon dry mustard for
more traditional yellow color)

Combine all ingredients. Warm over medium heat until warmed through, but do not boil.

Yield: 3/4 cup (enough for 4 poached eggs).

Compare the nutrients:

Per serving	Traditional	Light Version
Calories	473	219
Fat	38.3 g	6.7 g
Cholesterol	450 mg	20 mg

VARIATIONS ON THIS THEME:

EGGS OSCAR

Layer steamed, fresh asparagus spears, 1/4 cup cooked lump crab meat, the "poached" egg, and top with Mock Hollandaise.

EGGS SARDOU

Layer cooked fresh or frozen spinach (drained and patted dry with paper towels), chopped artichoke bottoms, "poached" egg, and top with Mock Hollandaise.

EGGS FLORENTINE

Layer cooked fresh or frozen spinach (drained and patted dry with paper towels), a fresh tomato slice, "poached" egg, and top with Mock Hollandaise Sauce.

EGGS NORTHWEST

Layer arugula leaves, smoked salmon, "poached" egg, and top with Mock Hollandaise Sauce.

EGGS WITH WILD MUSHROOMS

Layer sauteed mixture of sauteed mushrooms, onion, and garlic (shiitakes or morels are a real treat, if available), "poached" egg, topped with Mock Hollandaise.

STRATA - LAYERS OF FLAVOR

This is another dish that innkeepers love to make variations of ... because it is hearty, tasty, and most of all it MUST be prepared ahead of time. Therefore, morning preparation for breakfast is simplified (and the innkeeper might even get to enjoy a cup of coffee with her guests while it is baking).

Here are a couple of incarnations of this delightful and versatile dish. Feel free to add or subtract ingredients while adhering to the basic recipe, according to your own whim (or what you happen to have on hand in the refrigerator!).

RAISIN BREAD-PORK STRATA

3/4 pound lean ground pork
1/4 teaspoon rubbed sage
1/4 teaspoon dried thyme
1/8 teaspoon marjoram
1/8 teaspoon black pepper
1 1/4 cup egg substitute
1 cup skim milk
1/8 teaspoon ground red pepper
6 (1 ounce) slices whole wheat raisin bread, cut in
   half diagonally
1/4 cup (1 ounce) grated low fat sharp cheddar cheese

Combine first 5 ingredients in a non-stick skillet and brown pork; drain and pat dry with paper towels. Combine egg, milk, and red pepper and stir well. Add cooked pork to this mixture. Spray a 9-inch pie plate with cooking spray and arrange 6 of the half-slices of bread in the bottom. Pour half of pork mixture over bread. Repeat layers. Top with cheese. Bake at 350° for 20-30 minutes, or until "set" and cheese is lightly browned. Remove from oven and let it sit for 5 minutes, then cut into 4 wedges.

Yield: 4 hearty servings.

DEBBIE'S "MONTE CRISTO" STRATA

Debbie Leatherman, our assistant innkeeper, is a very talented and creative person. Not only is she a wonderful chef, but she has an eye for crafts and antiques that has drawn her into opening her own little shop. Artfully arranged, her shop features everything from lovely country antiques to hand-crafted jewelry and clothing which integrate antique quilts and ornaments. Her ability to artfully combine a variety of elements is demonstrated in this recipe which she developed, also. It looks pretty and tastes great!

We have made this dish in a large, jelly-roll style baking pan with a single layer of bread topped with the melange of toppings and baked for 30 minutes. We then slice the tray into 12 slices and serve each guest two slices.

You may either prepare the recipe as suggested here or follow the more typical strata format of making two layers of bread.

> 12 slices stone-ground whole wheat bread, crusts
>   removed
> 2 cups egg substitute
> 2 cups skim milk
> 1 tablespoon spicy, dijon-style mustard
> 1/4 teaspoon salt
> 1/4 teaspoon ground black pepper
> 1 pound turkey bacon, microwaved to a crunchy, easily
>   crumbled stage
> 12 slices lean, boiled ham, cubed
> 2 cups shredded low fat cheddar cheese, mozzarella, or
>   Swiss (or any combination of them)
> 1 bunch green onions, chopped
> Herb blend

In a bowl, whisk together the milk, eggs, mustard, salt, and pepper. Spray large, jelly roll style baking tray with cooking spray. Place the slices of bread tightly together in the bottom of the tray. Decorate the top of the bread with the meats, cheeses and onion. Sprinkle with dried herb or fresh herb blend. Slowly pour the egg mixture over the casserole to thoroughly moisten the bread. Cover with aluminum foil and refrigerate at least 2 hours, or overnight.

Preheat oven to 350° and bake the strata uncovered 45 minutes. Remove from the oven and let stand for 5 minutes before slicing into 12 squares and serving. Garnish with a green onion curl or fresh sprig of herb.

Yield: 12 servings.

STRATA ITALIANO

A nice rendition of this dish, especially in mid summer, when garden fresh tomatoes and basil are available.

6 slices stone-ground, whole wheat bread
3 cloves garlic minced
1 onion, diced
1 zucchini (small), diced
1/2 cup fresh mushrooms, sliced
3 tomatoes, peeled and chopped
2 teaspoons olive oil
2 cups egg substitute
1 cup skim milk
1/4 teaspoon each, salt and pepper
6 ounces shredded lowfat mozzarella cheese
1/8 cup grated Parmesan cheese
1 bunch each fresh basil and oregano (may use
**   1 tablespoon dried if fresh not available)**

Sauté garlic and onion in olive oil. Add tomatoes, zucchini, mushrooms and herbs and sauté briefly until just tender. Set aside. Spray 8x11-inch baking dish with cooking spray. Lay bread slices in bottom of dish. Beat eggs, milk, and salt/pepper. Pour egg mixture over bread and top with layer of vegetable mixture, then cheeses. Cover and refrigerate overnight. Bake uncovered in a 350° oven for 45 minutes or until lightly browned and puffy.

Yield: 8 servings.

TAYLOR'S STORE LOW-FAT CRUSTLESS QUICHE
SMOKED TURKEY AND CHEDDAR

Who says "real men don't eat quiche"?! Our most "man-ly" of men guests love this recipe. This heart-healthy rendition of the French egg and cheese pie is accomplished by omitting the fatty crust, using egg substitute in lieu of eggs, and blenderizing cottage cheese to add a special richness usually achieved with heavy cream. You can add any combination of lean meats, vegetables, herbs, or low fat cheeses. Some of my favorites include: spinach, mushrooms, onions, and mozzarella cheese with fresh parsley, dill, chives, and nutmeg (sort of a Greek treatment); turkey bacon, green pepper, tomato, garlic, mozzarella, and fresh basil (a touch Italian); and turkey ham, salsa, and cheddar with fresh cilantro (Tex-Mex-style).

We bake and serve these little quiches in individual 8-ounce fluted tart dishes (ours are handmade by the local Emerson Creek Pottery), but you can just as easily make a large one in a pie pan or large tart pan and cut it up to serve.

> 2 cups egg substitute (equivalent to 8 eggs)
> 1 cup lowfat cottage cheese
> 1/2 cup bread crumbs (may used herbed ones)
> 1/2 cup smoked turkey breast, cubed
> 1/2 cup lowfat cheddar cheese, grated
> 4 green onions, minced
> Salt, pepper, herbs to taste

Spray tart pans with cooking spray. Sprinkle bread crumbs on bottom and sides. Blenderize egg substitute and cottage cheese until smooth and creamy. With blender running, add dash of salt and pepper to taste.

Divide chopped turkey breast amongst the six individual tart pans (or spread it over the bottom of one large pan). Ladle 1/2 cup of egg/cheese mixture into each tart pan. Sprinkle each with grated cheese and minced green onion. If fresh or dried herbs are available, they may be sprinkled on top as well.

Bake in 350° oven for 20-30 minutes, or until set. Serve immediately.

Yield: 6 servings.

BAKED EGGS DU JOUR

Yet another dish that has as many possible variations as there are days in the week. You can vary the ingredients that complement the egg, or you can vary the container in which the egg is baked. Some of our favorites follow to whet your appetite for experimentation on your own.

THE BASIC BAKED EGG

For each serving:
1/2 cup egg substitute
Salt/pepper
1 teaspoon skim milk (or lowfat buttermilk) - optional

Preheat oven to 325°. Spray a 3-inch ramekin or 6 ounce custard dish with cooking spray. Pour in egg, sprinkle with salt/pepper. Bake for 10 minutes or until egg is just set. Serve immediately.

Alternatively, you can microwave these easy egg dishes. Just cover ramekins loosely with wax paper and microwave on HIGH for 1 - 2 minutes, turning once during cooking. The length of cooking time depends on your microwave... you'll have to test it out. If overcooked, the eggs will turn "green" ... not harmful, but unappetizing to all but fans of Dr. Suess' "Green Eggs and Ham"!

MONDAY'S EGG - ITALIAN STYLE

Spread 1 tablespoon marinara sauce in the bottom of ramekin. Add egg substitute. Top with 1/8 teaspoon olive oil, 1/2 teaspoon grated Parmesan cheese, a sprinkling of shredded mozzarella cheese, and 1/4 teaspoon chopped fresh parsley leaves.

TUESDAY'S EGG - CHEESY

Follow basic recipe. Add 1 tablespoon grated low fat cheddar, Swiss, or even feta cheese.

WEDNESDAY'S EGG - SMOKED TURKEY OR HAM

After spraying ramekin, place a chopped slice of smoked turkey or lean boiled ham in the bottom. Top with egg and bake as suggested.

THURSDAY'S EGG - AUX FINES HERBES

Put 1 teaspoon finely chopped fresh parsley and 1/2 teaspoon each dried thyme and marjoram (or any mixture of herbs you like in the bottom of each ramekin before adding egg.

FRIDAY'S EGG - BAKED IN A FRESH TOMATO

Cut the top off of a large fresh tomato and carefully hollow out some of the meat (leaving at least a 1/4-inch around the sides). Place egg and salt/pepper in tomato. Top with bread crumbs, and possibly a sprinkle of Parmesan cheese.

SATURDAY'S EGG - IN A PHYLLO NEST

Thaw phyllo dough according to package directions. Cut sheets into four pieces (may be stacked to do this). Spray each sheet with cooking spray (the "butter flavored" spray is nice in this recipe). Layer the four squares (per sheet) into an 8-ounce ramekin to create a "tulip-like" effect with the leaves. Sprinkle a small amount of grated cheese onto the bottom of the "tulip" and add the 1/2 cup egg substitute. Top with a sprinkling of pepper and herbs. Bake for 10-15 minutes or until phyllo is browned and egg is set. (This recipe cannot be done using the microwave method.)

SUNDAY'S EGG - TEX-MEX STYLE

One tablespoon salsa (homemade is best ... Pace's is the second best) in the bottom of ramekin with 1/2 cup egg substitute on top. Sprinkle with finely grated cheddar cheese in the last few minutes of baking. After cooking, I like to top with fresh, chopped cilantro, chopped black olives, and finely chopped green onions (and a little bit of chopped avocado ... I know the fat content is high ... but the extra flavor is worth it!).

MANOR POTATOES

The idea for this delicious combination came from a brunch at Le Peep, a popular restaurant in Dallas. I was there with my life-long best friend, Becca Klingel, for our 20th high school reunion. All of our other meals while there were Mexican food ... our shared culinary passion. The idea for this recipe was not the only wonderful memory I brought home from that trip!

4 medium potatoes, scrubbed, diced (unpeeled)
1 medium onion, finely chopped
1-2 cloves finely minced garlic
Salt and pepper to taste
1 (12-ounce) package turkey bacon, cooked and crumbled
1 cup grated lowfat cheddar cheese
1 1/2 cup egg substitute
3 chopped green onions

Combine potatoes, onion, and garlic in covered glass dish for microwave. Microwave on HIGH for 10-15 minutes, stirring and checking every 2-3 minutes, until potatoes are cooked (but not mushy). Season with salt and pepper to taste.

Spray skillet with cooking spray, preheat skillet over medium-low heat. Lightly whip egg substitute, dash of salt/pepper, and 1 tablespoon water together. When skillet is hot, add egg and gently scramble until fluffy and just cooked. Remove from heat.

Divide potato mixture evenly amongst 6 individual ramekins. (We use 6-inch baking dishes). Form a "nest" with a hole in the middle. Spoon 1/4 cup scrambled egg into the "nest". Top with crumbles of turkey bacon, green onions, and cheese.

Put baking dishes in a warm (250°) oven until cheese melts (5 minutes or less). Serve immediately.

Yield: 6 servings.

OMELETTE ROULADE

This version of an omelette is lower in cholesterol than the usual omelette because of the addition of the white sauce. The recipe serves 6 people; therefore, using real eggs (including yolks) results in a mere 170 mg of cholesterol per serving which is well below the recommended daily intake. It can be made with any combination of ingredients as filling. Fresh herbs may also be added, and a sprig of herb used as garnish.

Dried bread crumbs
1/4 cup margarine
1/2 cup all-purpose flour
2 cups skim milk
4 eggs, separated
1 cup low fat shredded cheddar cheese
1 teaspoon Worcestershire sauce
1/2 teaspoon salt
Dash red pepper sauce
12 slices turkey bacon, cooked and crumbled
1 small onion, minced (1/3 cup)
2 cups chopped fresh spinach
Garnish: 1/2 cup chopped tomato
   1/4 cup non-fat plain yogurt cheese

Preheat oven to 400°. Spray 15x10x1-inch jelly-roll pan; line with wax paper, and spray paper and sides of pan. Sprinkle with bread crumbs, tapping out excess.

Melt margarine in medium saucepan over medium heat. Whisk in flour and cook 2 minutes. Gradually stir in milk. Bring to boil, stirring constantly. Reduce heat and simmer 1 minute. Remove from heat and stir in egg yolks, cheese, Worcestershire, salt and red-pepper sauce.

Beat egg whites in mixer bowl until stiff but not dry. Fold 1/3 of egg whites into the cheese mixture, then fold in remaining whites. Spread evenly in prepared pan. Sprinkle with bacon and onion. Bake 18-20 minutes, until puffed and golden.

Arrange spinach on top, then roll up from long side, jelly-roll fashion, peeling wax paper off as you roll. Cut into 12 slices. Arrange plates with 2 slices each, topped with chopped tomatoes and yogurt cheese.

Yield: 6 servings.

CHILIES RELLENOS CASSEROLE

Most of the lovely flower arrangements, wreaths, needlework pillows, and table centerpieces that grace The Manor are the handiwork of our talented B&B hostess, Nancy Crow. Nancy's artistic ability extends to making guests feel immediately "at home" on their arrival, with her easy sense of humor and genuine hospitality. Another of her great attributes is that she is a Texan! She and I love to share reflections on the Lone Star State ... one of our fondest being the love of Mexican food.

This is not a recipe I have served our B&B guests, being sensitive to the fact that chilies at breakfast are not traditional in Virginia. However, I did want to include it for those of you who, like me, feel like that hot/spicy twang is just the thing to get the day going. It also makes a great brunch or supper dish.

1 cup egg substitute
3/4 cup skim milk
3/4 cup all-purpose flour
1/2 teaspoon salt
1/2 cup chopped onion
2 (7-ounce) cans whole green chilies, drained
8 slices (1 ounce each) Monterey Jack cheese,
    cut in halves
Optional garnishes: Yogurt cheese (or low fat sour
    cream), sliced green onions, sliced ripe olives,
    guacamole (sorry, I don't know of any way to
    make that low-fat ... but the indulgence is worth
    it to me), and lots of fresh salsa

Preheat oven to 350°. Combine egg substitute, milk, flour, and salt in blender and process until smooth and frothy. Spray small skillet with cooking spray, sauté onion until tender. Pat chilies dry with paper towels. Slit each chili lengthwise and carefully remove seeds. Place 2 halves of cheese and 1 tablespoon onion in each chili; reshape chilies to cover cheese.

Place chilies in single layer in greased 13x9-inch baking dish. Pour the egg/milk/flour mixture over chilies.

Bake 20-25 minutes or until topping is puffed and knife inserted in center comes out clean. Broil 4 inches below heat 30 seconds or until topping is golden brown. Serve with desired garnishes.

Yield: 4 servings.

BREAKFAST MEATS LOWER IN FAT

BREAKFAST MEATS LOWER IN FAT

In the "old days" (B.C.: before cholesterol) meat was considered an essential part of every meal. Because its availability was not as widely spread before modern refrigeration and marketing techniques, it was also a symbol of modern American affluence to have meat on the table with every meal. Bacon and eggs for breakfast, ham sandwich for lunch, and a big, juicy steak for dinner described a typical American meal plan, B.C.

Research in the past 30 years has shown us that we do not need as much protein in our diets as we thought we did. It has also provided evidence that meats, which are high in saturated fats and cholesterol, contribute to the development of atherosclerosis and heart disease. Thus, many people have chosen to completely eliminate meats of any sort from their diets. Many more have simply chosen to limit their intake of meats to the leaner meats, in smaller portions and less frequently.

At The Manor At Taylor's Store, we are happy to accommodate those on a completely vegetarian diet ... and have plenty of delicious dishes that don't involve meat at all. But, believing in moderation in all things, we also do offer several breakfast meats and meat dishes ... which feature lower fat than their traditional counterparts.

Occasionally, we'll simply serve slices of Canadian bacon, lean boiled ham, or turkey ham, grilled with a sprinkling of ground cloves. An attractive way to present thinly sliced smoked turkey breast or lean ham is to create little "rosettes". Simply crinkle up thinly sliced meat in your hand and place two per serving in muffin tins. Bake them in the oven for 10 minutes at 350° to "ruffle" the edges.

Following are some other recipes that we use to offer our guests variety and a lower-than-usual-fat content. While commercially prepared sausages contain a very high calorie: fat ratio (example: 265 calories with 21.6 grams of fat ... for 75% content), these sausage recipes are significantly lower in calorie: fat content. Each of these recipes has between 56-124 calories/serving and each contains less than 5 grams of fat (thus, the percentage of fat is cut almost in half, to as low as 23%). So, if you wish to indulge in sausage for breakfast occasionally, here are some "guilt-free" ways to do so.

SPICY HOMEMADE SAUSAGE

1 pound lean ground pork
1 teaspoon rubbed sage
1/2 teaspoon freshly ground pepper
1 clove of pressed garlic
1/4 teaspoon onion powder
1/4 teaspoon ground mace
1/8 teaspoon ground allspice
1/8 teaspoon salt
Dash of ground cloves

Combine all ingredients in a large mixing bowl; mix thoroughly. Shape into 12 small patties. Cook in a large skillet coated with cooking spray over medium heat until browned on both sides.

Yield: 6 servings (105 calories/serving).

PEPPERED TURKEY SAUSAGE

1/2 medium-sized green bell pepper
1/2 medium-sized red bell pepper
1 pound ground turkey
1 teaspoon Szechwan peppercorns
1/4 teaspoon ground ginger
1 tablespoon soy sauce (may use low sodium)
3-4 feet pork sausage casing

Position knife blade in food processor bowl, add bell peppers. Pulse until peppers are chopped. Add turkey, peppercorns, ginger, and soy sauce and process all until well combined.

Rinse pork casing in cold water, allowing water to run through casing until salt is removed; drain well. Tie 1 end of casing securely with string. Insert a large wide-mouth tip into a large pastry bag. Fill bag with sausage mixture. Slip open end of casing over tip of bag. Pipe sausage mixture into casing, using hand to force mixture evenly into casing. Tie end of casing. Twist sausage into 8 equal links; tie between links with string.

Place links in large skillet; add water to a depth of 1 inch. Place skillet over high heat; bring to a boil. cover, reduce heat, and cook over medium heat 15-20 minutes, turning occasionally. Remove from heat; set sausage aside, and discard water. Wipe skillet dry with a paper towel. Coat it with cooking spray and return links to skillet to cook until browned.

Yield: 8 links (4-inch) (about 56 calories each).

BEEF COUNTRY SAUSAGE

1 1/2 pounds ground chuck
1/2 pound lean ground veal
1/2 cup minced green bell pepper
1/2 cup fine, dry bread crumbs
2 tablespoons brandy
1 teaspoon mustard seeds
2 teaspoons onion powder
1 teaspoon garlic powder
1 teaspoon dried whole basil
1 teaspoon dried whole oregano
1 teaspoon ground cumin
1 teaspoon red pepper
1 teaspoon chili powder
1/2 teaspoon cinnamon
1/2 teaspoon salt

Combine all ingredients in a large bowl; stir well. Shape mixture into 2 rolls, 9 inches long x 2 inches in diameter. Wrap rolls in 2 (36x15-inch) thicknesses of dampened cheesecloth, and tie ends securely with string. Cover each roll with heavy duty plastic wrap, and chill at least 8 hours.

Remove plastic wrap, and place rolls in a 10x8x2-inch baking dish. Insert a meat thermometer into the center of 1 roll. Bake at 300° for 1 hour and 20 minutes or until thermometer registers 170°. Cool in refrigerator at least 2 hours.

To serve, remove cheesecloth and cut into slices.

Yield: 32 (1/2-inch) slices (about 62 calories each).

CHICKEN-CARROT SAUSAGE

1/2 pound carrots, scraped and sliced
2 tablespoons diced pimento
1/4 cup fresh parsley sprigs, packed
2 green onions
1 pound boned, skinned chicken breast halves
2 tablespoons olive oil
1 tablespoon water
1 tablespoon white wine
Worcestershire sauce
1 teaspoon dried tarragon
1/2 teaspoon celery seeds
1/8 teaspoon salt
1/4 teaspoon pepper
3-4 feet pork sausage casing

Cook carrots in a small amount of boiling water until tender. Drain carrots and set aside.

Position knife blade in food processor bowl; add pimento, parsley, and green onions. Pulse until minced. Add carrots to processor bowl, process until blended. Place mixture in a small bowl.

Add chicken to processor bowl and process until finely chopped. Add vegetable mixture to processor and process until blended. Add olive oil and next 6 ingredients to processor bowl, process until blended.

Rinse pork casing in cold water, allowing water to run through casing until salt is removed; drain well. Tie one end of casing securely with string. Insert a large, wide-mouth tip into a large pastry bag. Fill bag with sausage mixture. Sip open end of casing over tip of bag. Pipe sausage mixture into casing, using hand to force mixture evenly into casing. Tie end of casing. Twist sausage into 8 equal links; tie between links with string.

Place links in a large skillet; add water to a depth of 1-inch. Place skillet over high heat; bring to a boil. Cover, reduce heat, and cook over medium heat 10-15 minutes, turning occasionally. Remove from heat; set sausage aside, discard water.

Wipe skillet dry with paper towel. Coat skillet with cooking spray. Return sausage links to skillet and cook over medium heat until browned.

Yield: 8 (3-inch) links (about 125 calories each).

TURKEY SAUSAGE PATTIES

1 pound ground turkey
1 1/2 teaspoons oregano
1 1/2 teaspoons sage
2 teaspoons fennel seed
1 teaspoon freshly ground pepper
2 teaspoons salt
1/4 cup Tamari or soy sauce
1/2 teaspoon cayenne
2 tablespoons minced garlic
2 tablespoons Dijon mustard
2 teaspoons ground allspice
1/4 cup safflower oil

Mix all ingredients. Cover and refrigerate overnight. Form into patties and fry in non-stick pan.

Yield: 16 small patties, 8 servings.

CANADIAN BACON WITH CURRANT GLAZE

1 tablespoon brown sugar
1 teaspoon cornstarch
Dash of nutmeg
1/2 cup orange juice
2 tablespoons currants
10 slices lean Canadian bacon

Combine first 3 ingredients in a 2 cup glass measure. Gradually add orange juice, stirring well. Add currants, and microwave at HIGH 2-3 minutes or until slightly thickened, stirring after 1 1/2 minutes; set aside.

Arrange bacon, overlapping slices in a circular pattern around the edge of a 9-inch pie plate; pour orange juice mixture over bacon. Cover with wax paper, and microwave at HIGH 1 1/2 - 2 minutes or until bacon is thoroughly heated, rotating pie plate a quarter-turn after 1 minute.

Yield: 5 servings (about 84 calories per 2 slices and 1 tablespoon currant glaze).

VEGETARIAN SAUSAGE

We attempt to meet whatever special dietary needs our guests may have, from diabetics to vegan-vegetarians. This sausage (or, more appropriately, soy-sage) is a nice accompaniment to a breakfast of whole grains and fruits for those who prefer no meat. It can be cooked, refrigerated, and reheated before serving.

8 ounces tofu, mashed (1 cup)
1/4 cup wheat germ
2 tablespoons dried whole wheat bread crumbs
2 tablespoons sunflower seeds, finely ground
1/2 teaspoon dried sage
1/2 teaspoon dried thyme
1 clove garlic, minced
1/4 teaspoon salt

Combine all ingredients in a bowl and knead together with your hands until thoroughly mixed. Using 1 tablespoon at a time, squeeze into 2-inch long links. Place in steamer basket, set over boiling water, and steam 15 minutes. They may be refrigerated at this point. To serve, brown under a broiler or spray a skillet with cooking spray and brown over medium high heat.

Yield: 12 links, 4 servings.

THE COLONIAL GARDEN

Upon arrival at The Manor one of the first sights to captivate the visitor is the beautiful white gazebo surrounded by geometric brick walkways, between the house and the carriage house. The raised parterre beds are planted with herbs, flowers, shrubs, trees, and ground covers that would have been appropriate to the 18th and 19th centuries in this area. Teak benches are strategically placed to create comfortable spots for guests to read, relax, converse, or just enjoy the garden.

After having studied Colonial gardens, visited several of the historic gardens throughout Virginia, and worked and re-worked designs, Lee developed the garden plan. The brick work is laid in a pattern which (from above) resembles an acanthus flower, an early symbol of hospitality.

As with the development of The Manor in general, the creation of the garden has been (and continues to be) educational, challenging, and ever-evolving. It is our hope that our frequent guests will enjoy that process along with us.

SOUTHERN SAUSAGE GRAVY

No respectable Southern breakfast cookbook would omit a recipe for Sausage Gravy. Unlike the traditional recipe for this dish, this recipe has less than 20 milligrams of cholesterol/serving. Served over the Whole Wheat Biscuits in the "Bread" section of this book with the "Not Exactly Fried Apples", it makes a satisfying "country breakfast" in the Virginia tradition.

> **1 pound turkey sausage (you may use the earlier recipe for Turkey Sausage Patties as the base for this)**
> **1/2 cup margarine**
> **2/3 cup flour**
> **6 1/2 cups skim milk**
> **1/2 teaspoon salt**
> **1 teaspoon freshly ground pepper**
> **1/4 teaspoon Italian seasoning**

Spray a large nonstick skillet with non-stick spray. Brown sausage in skillet, stirring until it crumbles. Remove sausage from skillet, drain in colander, pat dry with paper towels. Wipe pan drippings from skillet. Melt margarine in skillet; add flour, stirring until smooth. Cook 1 minute, stirring constantly. Gradually add milk; cook over medium, heat, stirring constantly, until thickened and bubbly. Stir in seasonings and sausage. Cook until thoroughly heated, stirring constantly.

Yield: 8 servings (1 biscuit with 1/3 cup gravy).

COUNTRY TERRINE

This elegant dish, cousin to a paté, may be served for breakfast with crusty, whole grain bread and fresh fruit. It would be just as appropriate, with toast points, served as an appetizer with a glass of fine red wine.

1 1/2 pounds lean ground pork
2 tablespoons grated lemon rind
2 tablespoons lemon juice
5 cloves garlic, finely chopped
1 1/2 teaspoons dried thyme leaves
1/2 teaspoon salt
1 teaspoon ground coriander
1/2 teaspoon ground black pepper
1 10-ounce package frozen, chopped spinach
3 slices turkey bacon
Parsley for garnish

In a food processor, with the chopping blade, combine the pork, lemon rind and juice, garlic, thyme, salt, coriander, and pepper. Process until the mixture is finely ground. Cover tightly and refrigerate at least 2-4 hours. During this time, leave frozen spinach out at room temperature to thaw.

Before baking, drain spinach in colander and squeeze it very dry with paper towels. Fold this into the meat mixture.

Heat the oven to 325°. Spray a 1 1/2-quart round or oval terrine with cooking spray. Arrange the 3 slices of turkey bacon in the bottom. Pack in the meat-and-spinach mixture. Cover the terrine tightly with aluminum foil that has been sprayed with cooking spray. Bake the terrine 1 1/2 hours, or until a meat thermometer inserted in the center registers 170° and the juices are clear. Cool the terrine 30 minutes on wire rack. Pour off and discard the juices.

Cover the terrine tightly with aluminum foil. Place a plate on top and weight the meat with heavy cans or jars. Refrigerate at least 6 hours or overnight.

Slice and serve garnished with parsley.

Yield: 12 servings.

WHAT'S A JELLICLE CAT?

"Jellicle Cats have cheerful faces,
Jellicle Cats have bright green eyes;
They like to practise their airs and graces
And wait for the Jellicle Moon to rise". - T.S. Eliot

The inn cats are notorious for their humorous stunts. All named for cats from "Cats"...they certainly live up to their "jellicle" reputation. Grizabella, the solid gray matriarch, has been known to magically appear on the balcony betwen the Colonial and Toy Rooms. She's particularly prone to this stunt when guests are enjoying a snack while watching the sunset. She is also the cat whose green eyes have been known to startle guests enjoying a midnight soak in the hot tub. Her favorite activity is to join guests for a cozy nap on the hammock.

Guests taking a stroll to the ponds are accompanied by an experienced guide, Jezebelle, the sleek and shiny black cat. She trots a few paces ahead to show the way, then steers a wide path around the geese (territories were established years ago). When guests go out for a canoe ride, she insists on going along and posing as the masthead. If left behind, she paces the shoreline mewing until the canoe is paddled over and she can leap aboard!

Jenny-Any-Dots is the gray tabby cat whose domain is the gazebo in the Colonial garden. Her favorite activity is joining in on the champagne picnic that the balloon-riders enjoy after their flight. She's also been known to hang out at the cottage, and convince guests staying there that she is hungry and abandoned.

"So for Old Gumbie Cats let us now give three cheers -
On whom well-ordered households depend, it appears."

DESSERT FOR BREAKFAST

DESSERT FOR BREAKFAST

"Life is short ... eat dessert first" is one of Lee's favorite sayings. Philosophically, enjoyment of the present moment with knowledge of the uncertainty of the next moment is a zen-like approach to the day. Realistically, eating dessert first ... first thing in the morning ... is both celebratory and surprisingly nutritious. These recipes are proof that breakfast can be fun and still include all of the basic food groups. Likewise, served as dessert, they are evidence that a little sweet indulgence after a meal doesn't necessarily have to corrupt your heart-healthy diet. Enjoy!

BREAD PUDDINGS:
VARIATIONS ON A THEME

On our first date, Lee and I went to an afternoon concert and were planning to go out to dinner. He asked where I wanted to go ... I said it didn't matter ... he said he'd take me to his favorite place. We went to his apartment. I was amazed to see the table all set, fresh loaves of homemade French bread, and evidence of hours of preparation. Chopped vegetables were tossed into a salad and a luscious variety of seafoods and meats went into a Paella. To say I was impressed is an understatement! (I've wondered what would have happened if I'd said I wanted to go to a specific restaurant ... fate is interesting!)

After a lovely meal, Lee proceeded to "whip up" a whiskey sauce to top a delectable bread pudding. He had gotten the recipe from a favorite restaurant in New Orleans. Needless to say, I married the man!

Bread pudding makes a lovely breakfast item, served with any number of toppings or with a variety of additional ingredients added. This is a lowfat recipe, using the egg substitute, in which I challenge any eater to detect the absence of egg yolk by taste. I would reserve the real whiskey or rum sauce for an evening dessert, but a suitable breakfast substitute is the Rum Sauce here. Also, any of the fruit toppings in the Griddle Cake section are nice with the Bread Pudding.

When we were travelling in England, we were served a dessert called "Summer Pudding" which was basically a bread pudding with lots of fresh summer fruits and berries. This variation is a popular one with our B&B guests.

6 cups cubed bread, preferably day-old whole
    grain (you may use a sweetened bread, such as
    raisin or date bread for part or all)
2 cups egg substitute
4 cups skim milk
1/4 cup sugar
1 tablespoon vanilla extract
1/2 teaspoon nutmeg and/or cinnamon

    Optional Additional Ingredients (any or all):

1 cup raisins
1 teaspoon rum extract
1/2 cup chopped nuts
1 cup fresh berries, peaches, pears, etc., chopped

Put cubed bread in a large mixing bowl. Beat together egg substitute, milk, sugar, vanilla, and spice. Pour this mixture over bread cubes and mix well. Allow it to sit for at least 15 minutes so that bread absorbs liquid. At this point, you may add the raisins and/or nuts.

We prepare this recipe in individual 10-ounce ramekins, but the traditional preparation is to use a rectangular baking dish. Spray whichever you choose to use with cooking spray. Put the egg and bread mixture into baking dish(es). For summer pudding variation, fresh fruit should be put in the bottom of the baking dish before topping with egg mixture.

The baking dish(es) may be refrigerated overnight, if you are preparing this ahead of time for breakfast.

Preheat oven to 350°. Bake for 30-45 minutes, or until golden and toothpick inserted near center comes out clean. If you are making the large pan variation, allow it to cool for 10 minutes before serving. The individual variation may either be served in the ramekins, or removed to a plate. For the summer pudding variation, top with additional fresh fruit. Otherwise, a sprinkle of powdered sugar or the Rum Sauce below is an elegant presentation.

RUM SAUCE

2 cups confectioners' sugar
2 tablespoons evaporated skim milk
1 tablespoon rum extract

Mix together all ingredients and serve over hot bread pudding.

FRESH FRUIT TART

This was one of the first recipes I served guests when we opened the B&B. Over the years, I've refined the crust to further reduce fat ... but it still proves to be one of the prettiest and tastiest summer breakfast dishes we serve.

Pastry

1 cup stirred cake flour
2 tablespoons sugar, divided
1/4 cup margarine, cut into small pieces and chilled
2-3 tablespoons ice water

Combine flour and 1 tablespoon sugar in a large bowl; cut in margarine with a pastry blender until mixture resembles coarse meal and is pale yellow (about 3 1/2 minutes). Sprinkle ice water (1 tablespoon at a time) over surface; toss with a fork until dry ingredients are moistened and mixture is crumbly. (Do not form a ball). Gently press mixture into a 4-inch circle on heavy-duty plastic wrap, and chill 15 minutes. Roll dough, still covered, to a 13-inch circle. Then place dough in freezer 5 minutes or until heavy-duty plastic wrap can easily be removed. Fit dough into a 12-inch pizza pan (black metal pan works best,but a non-shiny pan or glass pie plate can be used), and remove plastic wrap. Fold edges under and flute. Prick bottom of pastry with a fork. Chill 15 minutes. Bake at 400° for 12 minutes or until lightly browned; cool completely on a wire rack.

Tart Topping

1 cup lowfat cottage cheese
2 tablespoons frozen orange juice concentrate, thawed
1 tablespoon sugar
2-3 cups sliced fresh fruit, such as strawberries, kiwi, blueberries, raspberries, banana, cantaloupe, etc.
2 tablespoons red currant jelly
2 teaspoons apricot preserves
1 teaspoon sugar
1/2 teaspoon Triple sec or other orange liqueur (optional)

Combine cottage cheese, orange juice, and 1 tablespoon sugar in blender or food processor and blend until very smooth and creamy. Spread this mixture evenly over the baked tart pastry. Arrange the sliced fruit decoratively on top of the cheese mixture.

In a small saucepan, combine jelly, preserves and 1 teaspoon sugar. Cook over medium heat until the mixture boils. Remove from heat and push mixture through a sieve to remove pulp. Add 1/2 teaspoon orange liqueur if desired. Allow this to cool slightly, but before it sets back up into a jelly-like consistency, drizzle it over the fruit-topped tart.

Yield: 8 servings.

BREAKFAST FRUIT CUSTARD

Custards are moist, gentle, "comfort foods". Most people associate them with grandmothers and being taken care of by a loving person in the kitchen. Exactly the feeling we hope to evoke in our B&B guests when we serve them for breakfast. Besides their delicious taste, they are basically a complete, healthful breakfast by themselves ... made of morning ingredients, such as dairy products, eggs, and fruits.

Traditionally, egg custards owe their creamy, rich nature to a hefty dose of fat via egg yolks and heavy cream. However, believe it or not, the same texture and taste is achievable, minus most of the cholesterol. Try this recipe, close your eyes, and imagine Grandma serving it to you.

1 cup fresh berries, chopped peaches, nectarines
    or any combination thereof
1 cup lowfat cottage cheese
1 cup lowfat yogurt
1 cup skim milk
1/2 teaspoon lemon zest
1 teaspoon vanilla extract
2 eggs (may use 1/2 cup egg substitute, but in this recipe
    eggs work best and since it serves 8 people, each
    person doesn't get more than the equivalent of
    1/4 egg in cholesterol (less than 60 milligrams)
1/2 cup sugar
1/2 cup flour
1/2 teaspoon salt
2 cups of additional chopped fresh fruit/berries

Preheat oven to 425°. Spray eight 6-ounce custard cups with cooking spray. Divide the fruit into the cups.

In a blender, combine the cottage cheese, yogurt, and milk and blend until smooth. Add lemon zest, vanilla, and eggs and blend. Add sugar, flour, and salt; blend until smooth.

Divide the mixture over the fruit in the cups. Bake for 20-25 minutes, until set and lightly golden. To serve, run a knife around the edges of the custard cups; invert and unmold the custard onto plates. Top with additional chopped fresh fruit/berries. If you want an extra special presentation, a puddle of strawberry coulis (recipe in the fruit section of this book) is a nice bed for the custard.

Yield: 8 servings.

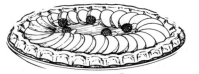

NEW ZEALAND PAVLOVA

To celebrate my 40th birthday, Lee and I journeyed to far away New Zealand. We camped and explored that magnificent country from the South Island to the North Island. The scenic beauty - mountains, glaciers, clear rivers, rocky coastlines, and unspoiled wilderness - is truly some of the world's grandest. The warm "Kiwi" hospitality is equally impressive!

Our dear "Kiwi" friends, John and Sally Stephenson, sent us this recipe. Pavlova is the "national dessert" of New Zealand. Appropriately named for a graceful Russian ballerina, it is light and airy with elegant swirls of meringue. Decorated with kiwi fruit and strawberries, both the presentation and the delicious taste are a wonderful surprise ... at breakfast or dessert.

Now a staple in American supermarkets, the kiwi fruit has an interesting history. It was first introduced to New Zealand in 1906 by a German orchardist, and was known as Chinese gooseberry. As the fruit prospered, growers renamed it kiwi after their national bird (which is also brownish and fuzzy and doesn't fly). Due to tremendous popularity, U.S. growers planted their first vineyards in California during the sixties, and there is now commercial planting in the South as well. The tangy-sweet kiwi fruit is an excellent source of vitamin C, potassium, and dietary fiber, and is free of sodium (and only 45 calories/each).

> **4 egg whites**
> **Few grains of salt**
> **3/4 cup powdered sugar**
> **1/2 teaspoon vanilla extract**
> **1 teaspoon vinegar**
> **1 teaspoon cornstarch**
> **Kiwi fruit, peeled & sliced**
> **Fresh strawberries, sliced**

Preheat the oven to 350° (the temperature is reduced for baking). Place a sheet of parchment paper on an oven tray. Brush lightly with melted butter and dust with a little cornstarch ... shake off excess.

Beat the egg whites to a foam with a rotary or electric beater, add the salt; beat to a stiff foam or until the peaks fold over when the beater is removed. Beat in the sugar: add 1 tablespoon at a time; beat until the mixture is stiff and the peaks stand up when the beater is removed. Add the vanilla, vinegar, and cornstarch. Blend thoroughly.

Spoon the meringue mixture onto prepared tray, forming a 9-inch circle. Reduce oven to 275°, and bake at this temperature for 15 minutes, then further reduce heat to 250° and continue baking for 1 hour. Allow to cool in oven.

When cool, remove from oven and place on a flat serving plate. The "official" recipe calls for topping with whipped cream before decorating with fruit. As an alternative, you can blend your own low-fat vanilla cream. Process together in blender until smooth and creamy:

1/2 cup lowfat cottage cheese
1/2 cup nonfat plain yogurt
3 tablespoons sugar
1/2 teaspoon vanilla extract

Spread this mixture evenly over the top of the Pavlova. Peel and slice several kiwi fruit and fresh strawberries. Arrange the fruit according to your own creativity. Serve immediately.

Yield: 4-6 generous slices.

RAINBOW RICOTTA TARTS

Phyllo pastry makes any dish special! This recipe is lovely as a summer breakfast or dessert.

4 sheets phyllo dough, thawed
Butter-flavored vegetable cooking spray
1/2 cup part-skim ricotta cheese
2 tablespoon honey
2 (1/2-inch thick) fresh pineapple slices,
   each cut into quarters
1/4 cup fresh blueberries
4 fresh strawberries, halved
2 kiwi fruit, peeled and sliced
1 medium seedless orange, peeled, sectioned

Working with 2 phyllo sheets at a time, lightly spray each sheet with cooking spray, placing one on top of the other.

Cut into 6 (6x5-inch) squares. Repeat procedure with remaining phyllo sheets. Place 3 stacks of squares on top of one another; prick the center of each stack with a fork. Press into the bottom of 4 (6-ounce) custard cups.

Bake at 375° for 10 minutes, or until golden. Remove from cups, and cool completely on wire rack.

Combine cheese and honey in container of electric blender and process mixture until smooth. Spoon mixture evenly into shells. Place shells on a baking sheet and chill 15 minutes.

Divide fruit evenly among shells. Serve immediately.

Yield: 4 servings.

FRESH FRUIT CRISP

Fruit crisps are a classic dessert that enable you to take advantage of whatever fresh fruits are available. Our newest assistant innkeeper, Martha Garst, is also a newly-wed. Her husband, John, manages the largest commercial apple orchard in the region. We have an inside track to the best and freshest apples around! Apples, pears, peaches, and even strawberries, blueberries, or rhubarb really shine when prepared in this fashion. Topped with yogurt cheese (or frozen yogurt as dessert), a fruit crisp is an inviting dish!

5 cups peeled, chopped fresh fruit - individually
   or combined - apples, pears, peaches, blueberries,
   strawberries, raspberries, or lightly sugared rhubarb
1 teaspoon lemon juice
1 teaspoon vanilla extract
1 tablespoon sugar
1 tablespoon cornstarch
1/2 teaspoon cinnamon
1/2 teaspoon nutmeg
1/3 cup flour
1/3 cup regular oats, uncooked
2 tablespoons dark brown sugar
1/4 teaspoon cinnamon
2 tablespoons margarine (stick, chilled)

Combine fruit, lemon juice, vanilla in a large bowl. Combine cornstarch, 1/2 teaspoon cinnamon, nutmeg in small bowl; then add to fruit, tossing gently to coat all fruit.

Combine flour, oats, brown sugar, and 1/4 teaspoon cinnamon in a small bowl; cut in margarine with a pastry blender until mixture resembles coarse meal.

Spray an 8x10-inch baking dish with cooking spray. Spoon fruit mixture into baking dish. Sprinkle flour/oat mixture evenly over the fruit. Preheat oven to 400°. Bake crisp for 25 minutes or until browned and bubbly.

Yield: 6 servings.

GERMAN APRICOT STRUDEL

Our assistant innkeeper, Barbara Bell, is a native of Berlin, Germany. It is amazing how many of our guests are German-speaking and appreciate being able to converse in their native tongue. It provides that extra touch of hospitality that makes them feel "at home" at The Manor.

Strudel is a traditional German pastry served on special occasions for special friends. This version of strudel uses phyllo sheets, so it is easy enough to make often ... which is good for us, because special occasions and special friends are a daily event at The Manor!

8 sheets of phyllo dough, defrosted
Butter-flavored vegetable cooking spray
2 cups dried apricots, soaked in hot water
 for a few hours or overnight
1/4 cup honey
1 whole lemon (skin, pulp, everything
 but seeds), grated and pitted
1 whole orange (skin, pulp, everything
 but seeds), grated and pitted
1 cup crushed walnuts
1/2 teaspoon cinnamon
1 cup golden raisins
1/2 cup graham cracker crumbs
1/2 cup wheat germ
1 cup unsweetened shredded coconut
1/2 cup confectioners sugar
Juice of one lemon

Spray a 9x13-inch jelly roll pan with vegetable spray. Remove one sheet of phyllo from the pile and place it in the center of the pan; spray it lightly with the butter flavored vegetable cooking spray. Place a second sheet on top and spray again. Continue until all the sheets have been used.

Preheat the oven to 350°.

Make the apricot filling: drain the water from the soaked apricots. In a food processor, blend together the apricots, honey, and half the grated lemon and orange. Reserve the other half for use with the nut mixture.

Make the nut mixture: combine the walnuts, cinnamon, raisins, crumbs, wheat germ, coconut, and reserved grated lemon and orange.

Spray the center of the phyllo sheets. Sprinkle with half of the nut mixture and top with half of the apricot filling. Fold one-third of the dough over the center section. Spray, and sprinkle with the remaining nut mixture and remaining apricot filling. Fold the final third over the center section and spray top and sides well. The cake should measure 14x16 inches.

Place the roll on the jelly roll pan. With a sharp knife, make four slits in the strudel diagonally, but do not cut all the way through. Bake for 20 minutes, or until golden brown. Remove and cool slightly. In a small bowl, mix 1/2 cup confectioners sugar and lemon juice together and drizzle over the warm cake. Cut into slices, 1x3 inches.

Yield: 28 pieces.

CHILLED LEMON SOUFFLÉ

A most refreshing, elegant, and impressive breakfast/dessert is a chilled soufflé. With the sweetness and coolness of ice cream, the lightness of a mousse, and the decadence of an exotic dessert ... the Lemon Soufflé promises to delight. Best of all, this soufflé does not involve the usual egg yolks and whipped cream. The same result is achieved by using beaten egg whites and whipped non-fat milk. Served with fresh muffins, ruffled turkey ham, and fresh fruit ... ahhhh, the perfect antidote to a hot, sultry August morning!

> 6 thin lemon slices, halved
> 3 thin lemon slices, quartered
> 1 cup water, divided
> 2 envelopes unflavored gelatin
> 3/4 cup sugar, divided
> 1 tablespoon grated lemon rind
> 1/2 cup fresh lemon juice
> 2/3 cup instant nonfat dry milk powder
> 4 egg whites
> 1 tablespoon finely chopped pistachios
> Candied lemon rind strips for garnish

Cut a piece of aluminum foil long enough to fit around the soufflé dish you are using, allowing a 1 inch overlap; fold lengthwise into thirds (we prepare these in individual 6-ounce soufflé dishes, but you can also use a large 1-quart dish). Wrap foil around outside of dish, allowing it to extend 3 inches above rim to form a collar. Secure the foil with freezer tape. Arrange lemon slices along side of dish.

Place 2/3 cup water in a small, narrow glass or stainless steel bowl; freeze 25 minutes or until a 1/8-inch thick layer of ice forms on surface.

Sprinkle gelatin over remaining 1/3 cup water in a non-aluminum sauce pan; let stand 1 minute. Place over low heat; cook until gelatin dissolves, stirring constantly. Remove from heat; add 1/2 cup sugar, lemon rind, and lemon juice, stirring until sugar dissolves. Place in a bowl; cover and chill 25 minutes or until slightly thickened, stirring frequently.

Add milk powder to partially frozen water; beat at high speed of an electric mixer 5 minutes or until stiff peaks form. Set aside. Beat egg whites (at room temperature) in a large glass or stainless steel bowl at medium speed of an electric mixer about 1 minute or until soft peaks form. Add remaining 1/4 cup sugar, 1 tablespoon at a time, beating at high speed until stiff peaks form. (Do not overbeat.)

Gently stir 1/4 of the egg white mixture into lemon mixture. Gently fold milk powder mixture into lemon mixture. spoon mixture into prepared soufflé dish. Chill 4 hours, or overnight. Remove collar, and gently press finely chopped pistachios around sides of soufflé. Garnish with candied lemon rind strips, if desired.

Yield: 6 servings.

CHILLED RASPBERRY SOUFFLÉ

Follow the preceding recipe for preparation of soufflé dishes, making of gelatin mixture, making of whipped nonfat milk powder, and beating of egg whites. In place of sugar, lemon rind, and lemon juice added to the dissolved gelatin mixture, add raspberry puree:

4 cups fresh raspberries

Rinse raspberries, drain. Position knife blade in food processor bowl; add raspberries. Top with cover, and process 1 minute or until smooth. Strain mixture to remove seeds.

Gently stir 1/4 egg white mixture into raspberry mixture. Gently fold remaining egg white mixture into raspberry mixture. Gently fold milk powder mixture into raspberry mixture. Spoon mixture into prepared soufflé dishes. Chill 8 hours or overnight. Remove collar, and garnish soufflé with fresh raspberries, if desired.

Yield: 6 servings.

UP, UP, AND AWAY!

One of the most romantic and unique activities our guests enjoy is the opportunity to take flight in a hot air balloon from the back lawn of The Manor. Just after the sun comes up, guests congregate on the lawn to photograph and assist in the inflation of the balloon. Pilot Denny Laughlin (with years of experience flying balloons in Napa Valley before moving to Smith Mountain Lake) explains every step of the process and ensures the comfort and safety of all passengers. When the balloon is fully inflated, guests climb into the wicker basket... and take off with the breeze. Rising up, up, and over trees...drifting lazily over pastures and forests (and often over the lake)...and seeing the beauty of the world from a whole new perspective is a very special treat. There is a chase crew that follows along to bring guests and balloon back to The Manor after the flight. The grand finale is a champagne reception with a celebratory ceremony to commemorate the flight!

"A balloon flight brings a smile to your face, joy to your heart, and peace to your spirit". - Pilot Denny Laughlin

FOUR FRUIT ICE

Breakfast dessert ... a cool, refreshing ice or sorbet to finish off the hearty meal ... why not? This recipe can also be used as an "intermezzo" between courses for a special dinner.

1 3/4 cups water, divided
1/2 cup sugar
2 teaspoons grated lime rind
1 (20-ounce) can unsweetened pineapple tidbits, undrained
2 (16-ounce) packages unsweetened frozen whole strawberries, thawed
1 (16-ounce) package unsweetened frozen raspberries, thawed
1 tablespoon lime juice

Combine 1 1/4 cups water, sugar, and lime rind in a medium, non-aluminum saucepan; bring to a boil. Remove from heat, and pour into a small bowl. Let sugar mixture cool to room temperature.

Drain pineapple tidbits, reserving 1/4 cup juice; set both aside. Combine strawberries, raspberries, and remaining 1/2 cup water in a medium, non-aluminum saucepan; bring to a boil. Reduce heat, and simmer 7 minutes or until berries soften. Remove from heat. Position knife blade in food processor bowl; add berries and pineapple tidbits. Process until smooth. Press mixture through sieve into a large bowl; discard seeds. Add sugar mixture, 1/4 cup reserved pineapple juice, and lime juice, then stir well.

Position knife blade in processor bowl; add 2 cups mixture. Process until smooth. Pour mixture into 13x9x2-inch baking dish. Repeat procedure with remaining mixture; pour into baking dish, and stir well. Freeze mixture until it is firm, stirring occasionally.

Before serving, process mixture again in food processor (no more than half of the recipe at a time). Spoon fruit ice into serving dishes, garnish with a fresh raspberry or lime wedge.

Yield: 8 cups (serving size may vary - 1/4 cup is a nice "finishing" touch).

PEAR SORBET

When Lee and I were serving six-course gourmet dinners to our guests, this was the "intermezzo" course. Still a nice ending to a hearty breakfast.

1 (16-ounce) can pear halves in light syrup, drained
3 tablespoons lemon juice
1/2 teaspoon grated lemon rind

Position knife blade in food processor bowl; add all ingredients and process until smooth. Pour mixture into 8-inch square glass pan; freeze until almost firm. Break mixture into large pieces; place in processor bowl. Process several seconds or until fluffy but not thawed.

Scoop sorbet into individual sherbet or champagne glasses. Serve immediately.

Yield: 2 cups (1/4 cup serving is ample).

STEAMED PERSIMMON PUDDING

Persimmons grow wild at Taylor's Store, and if we time the harvest just right ... they are a marvelous surprise for B&B guests. Timing the harvest is very critical with persimmons. If eaten unripe, they are very astringent and result in an uncontrollable pucker on the face of the eater! However, if you wait until after the first frost, and then pick only the ones that feel soft to the touch and come off in your hand with no effort, you will be rewarded with a sweet burst of flavor. This persimmon pudding has become a Thanksgiving/Christmas tradition for us. Best of all, it can be made ahead and reheated, or even frozen.

1 cup pureed persimmons (put through
    a colander to remove seeds and skin)
2 teaspoons baking soda
8 tablespoons (1 stick) margarine
1 1/2 cups sugar
2 eggs (go ahead and use the real
    thing ... less than 1/4 egg yolk/serving)
1 tablespoon lemon juice
2 tablespoons rum
1 cup all-purpose flour
1 teaspoon cinnamon
1/2 teaspoon salt
1 cup chopped walnuts or pecans
1 cup raisins

Fill a kettle that is large enough to hold a 2-quart pudding mold with enough water to come halfway up the sides of the mold. Let the water come to a boil over medium heat while you are mixing the pudding batter. The mold must have a lid or be snugly covered with foil while steaming (a coffee can with plastic lid works well). Also there must be a rack or Mason jar ring of the bottom under the mold in the kettle to allow the water to circulate freely while the pudding is steaming. Spray the mold well with cooking spray.

Put the persimmon puree in a small bowl and stir in the baking soda. Set aside while mixing the other ingredients (the persimmon mixture will become quite stiff).

Cream the margarine with sugar. Add the eggs, lemon juice, and rum, and beat well. Add the flour, cinnamon, and salt, and stir to blend. Add the persimmon mixture. Beat until well mixed. Stir in the nuts and raisins.

Spoon the batter into the mold, cover, and steam for 2 hours. Remove from the kettle, and let rest for 5 minutes. Turn onto a rack to cool, or cool just a little and serve warm. Nice topped with "Sour Lemon Sauce" below.

Yield: 8 servings.

SOUR LEMON SAUCE

1 tablespoon cornstarch
1/4 cup sugar
1 cup orange juice
1 1/2 tablespoon lemon juice
1 teaspoon grated lemon zest
Pinch salt

Combine cornstarch and sugar in saucepan. Slowly whisk in orange juice. Cook, stirring, over low heat until the mixture is thickened and begins to boil. Stir in lemon juice, zest, and salt. Remove from the heat. Serve warm over pudding.

FRESH FRUIT SHORTCAKES

These butter-free versions of the classic fruit shortcake biscuits are delicious topped with fresh strawberries, peaches, or any combination of lovely summer fruits.

3 tablespoons sugar
1 teaspoon cinnamon
1 cup unbleached flour
1 cup whole wheat flour
1 tablespoon baking powder
1/3 cup canola oil
2/3 cup skim milk
4 cups fresh strawberries, peaches, or other
    summer fruits ... chopped and lightly sugared
1 cup vanilla yogurt cheese (see recipe for yogurt cheese)

Preheat oven to 475°. Mix 1 tablespoon sugar with 1/2 teaspoon of cinnamon in a small bowl. In another bowl, combine flours, remaining 1/2 teaspoon cinnamon, baking powder, and remaining 2 tablespoons sugar. Add oil and milk; stir until mixture readily leaves side of bowl and can be formed into a ball. Drop by tablespoons onto an ungreased baking sheet. Sprinkle with cinnamon/sugar mixture. Bake 10-12 minutes.

To serve, place hot shortcakes on individual plates, spoon fresh fruit onto each shortcake, and top with a dollop of the vanilla yogurt cheese.

Yield: 8 servings.

HOLIDAY TRIFLE

This traditional English dish was a favorite dessert when we served dinners to our guests. The lowfat sponge cake, fresh fruit, and lowfat pastry cream are appropriate components for a festive breakfast dish as well.

Sponge Cake

3 eggs, separated
1/2 cup plus 2 tablespoons sugar, divided
2 tablespoons water
1 teaspoon vanilla extract
1 cup sifted cake flour
1/8 teaspoon salt
1/2 teaspoon cream of tartar

Coat a 9-inch round cake pan with cooking spray; line bottom of pan with wax paper, and set aside.

Combine egg yolks and 1/2 cup sugar in a medium bowl; beat at high speed of an electric mixer 5 minutes. Add water, beating at low speed until well blended; beat at high speed 30 seconds. Stir in vanilla. Gently fold flour and salt into egg yolk mixture; set aside.

Beat egg whites (at room temperature) until foamy; add cream of tartar, and beat until soft peaks form. Add remaining 2 tablespoons sugar; beat until stiff but not dry. Fold egg whites into batter. Pour batter into prepared pan. Bake at 350° for 25 minutes or until center springs back when touched lightly. Cool 10 minutes in pan on wire rack. Remove from pan, and cool completely on rack.

Sherried Pastry Cream

1/4 cup sugar
2 tablespoons cornstarch
1 egg
2 cups evaporated skimmed milk
1/4 cup cream sherry
1/4 teaspoon vanilla extract

Sift together sugar and cornstarch in a medium bowl. Add egg; beat at high speed of an electric mixer 5 minutes. Bring milk to a boil over medium heat in medium saucepan, stirring constantly. Gradually stir about one fourth of hot milk into egg mixture; add to remaining hot milk, stirring constantly. Cook over medium heat 2 minutes or until mixture is thickened, stirring constantly. Remove from heat; let cool 5 minutes, stirring frequently. Stir in cream sherry and vanilla. Cool completely; cover and chill.

Building the Trifle

1 medium pineapple, peeled and cored
1/4 cup orange juice
3 cups halved fresh strawberries
3 medium seedless oranges, peeled, sectioned, halved
Basic Sponge Cake
Sherried Pastry Cream

Cut pineapple in half crosswise. With cut side down, cut one half into 8 wedges. Cut each wedge crosswise into 1/4-inch slices. Combine pineapple and orange juice in a bowl; toss well and set aside.

Cut Basic Sponge Cake in half horizontally, then cut each layer into 1/2-inch slices, then cut slices in half crosswise. Line the bottom of 12 individual trifle bowls (or one 3 quart straight sided glass bowl) with 1/3 of the sponge cake pieces.

Drain pineapple mixture, reserving liquid. Drizzle reserved liquid over sponge cake in bowls. Arrange 1/3 each of strawberries, oranges, and pineapple around lower edge of bowls over cake. Spoon 1/3 of Sherried Pastry Cream over fruit layer. Repeat procedure 2 more times with remaining ingredients. Cover and chill at least 8 hours. Garnish with a strawberry fan.

Yield: 12 servings.

TRIPLE CHOCOLATE TORTE FOR MY SWEETHEART

Chocolate is Lee's favorite food, so I had to include something chocolate in this cookbook. This recipe fills the bill in terms of being both very chocolate-y and very heart healthy (only 1 milligram cholesterol and 4 grams of fat/serving). At the B&B, we often celebrate guests' birthdays, anniversaries, and other special events. This triple chocolate torte is just the thing!

Chocolate Cake

1 cup plus 1 tablespoon sifted caked flour, divided
3/4 cup sugar plus 2 teaspoons, divided
1/3 cup unsweetened cocoa
1 teaspoon baking powder
1/2 teaspoon baking soda
1/8 teaspoon salt
1/2 cup water
1/4 cup vegetable oil
2 teaspoons vanilla extract
5 egg whites

Line a 15x10x1-inch jelly roll pan with aluminum foil, allowing foil to extend beyond ends of pan. Coat foil with cooking spray; dust with 1 tablespoon flour and set aside. Preheat oven to 325°.

Combine 3/4 cup cake flour, 1/4 cup plus 2 tablespoons sugar, cocoa, baking powder, baking soda, and salt in bowl; stir well. Make a well in the center of mixture. Combine water, oil, and vanilla; add to dry ingredients, stirring until blended. Set chocolate mixture aside.

Beat egg whites (at room temperature) in a large bowl until foamy. Add 1/4 cup plus 2 tablespoons sugar, 1 tablespoon at a time, beating until stiff peaks form. Fold one-third of egg white mixture into chocolate mixture; carefully fold in remaining egg white mixture and remaining 1/4 cup flour. Spoon into jelly roll pan, spreading evenly to sides of pan.

Bake at 325° for 25 minutes or until a toothpick inserted in center comes out clean. Cool 30 minutes in pan on wire rack. Invert jelly roll pan onto a baking sheet; remove pan, and carefully peel aluminum foil away from cake. Cut cake into 28 hearts, using a 2 1/2-inch heart-shaped cookie cutter (remaining cake is yours to "taste"...yum!).

Chocolate Ganache

1 cup semisweet chocolate chips
1/2 cup lowfat cottage cheese
1/2 cup nonfat plain yogurt
1 tablespoon espresso
1 tablespoon vanilla extract

In the top of a double boiler over simmering water, melt the chocolate until smooth. Remove from the heat and cool until just barely warm, stir in espresso; do not allow it to set.

Blenderize cottage cheese and yogurt together with vanilla until smooth and creamy. Place this mixture in a small mixing bowl and gradually whisk the warm chocolate in until thoroughly combined. May be refrigerated until ready to use.

Chocolate-Orange Sauce

1/3 cup sugar
1/3 cup unsweetened cocoa
1/4 cup water
2 tablespoons Grand Marnier
1/4 cup light-colored corn syrup
1 teaspoon vanilla extract

Combine sugar and cocoa in saucepan; stir well. Add water, stirring until smooth. Add liqueur and corn syrup; stir well. Place over medium heat; bring to boil, stirring constantly. Remove from heat; stir in vanilla. Pour sauce into bowl, cool, and refrigerate covered until ready for use.

Making the Heart-shaped Torte

Begin with one chocolate cake-heart, spread 1 teaspoon chocolate ganache on one side. Top with another cake-heart. Do this until you have all 14 "sandwiches" made. To serve, place each chocolate cake heart on an individual serving plate, spoon 1 tablespoon of Chocolate-Orange Sauce over heart, decorate with fresh slices of strawberry, if desired.

Yield: 14 tortes.

BREAKFAST IN A COOKIE

We serve our full breakfast in the formal dining room between 8:30-10, since most of our guests are on holiday and want a more leisurely start to their day than they are used to. However, we also have guests who are very early risers and head out to go fishing, hiking, or just exploring. We set up an early coffee pot for them in the guest kitchen, and leave them a nice plate of fresh fruit, a can of juice, and a couple of these delicious "Breakfast in a Cookie"s. Makes you feel like a kid to eat such a delicious treat for breakfast, and they are so tasty, you'd never suspect they're good for you, too!

1/2 cup canola oil
1/2 cup unsweetened applesauce
1/2 cup brown sugar
1/4 cup egg substitute
1 tablespoon vanilla extract
1 tablespoon orange juice
1 tablespoon lemon juice
1/2 cup oat bran
1/2 cup seven-grain cereal
1/2 cup all-purpose flour
1/2 cup whole wheat pastry flour
1 teaspoon baking soda
1/2 teaspoon salt
1 teaspoon ground cinnamon
1 teaspoon ground allspice
1 teaspoon ground ginger
1/2 teaspoon ground cloves
3 cups old fashioned oats
1 cup golden raisins
Optional: 1/4 cup unsweetened coconut and/or
    1/4 cup chopped walnuts (these items do add
    significant fat to the recipe)

Preheat oven to 350°. In a large mixing bowl, beat together with electric mixer oil, applesauce, and brown sugar. Add egg substitute, vanilla, orange juice, and lemon juice, then beat again. Sift together oat bran, 7-grain cereal, flours, baking soda, salt, and spices. Add these ingredients to the wet ingredients and mix well. Stir in oats. Fold in raisins (and other optional ingredients if you wish). Place cookie dough on ungreased cookie sheets by the tablespoonful. Bake for 15 minutes or until golden. Remove the cookies from the sheet immediately and cool completely.

Yield: 3 dozen large cookies.

BREAKFAST
CHEESES

BREAKFAST CHEESES

There's a good reason why photographers wanting their subjects to smile have them say "cheese"! This delicious food adds flavor and texture to every other food that it comes in contact with. Tasty food, smiling faces.

Choosing a low-fat diet does not mean that you have to give up this marvel of nature ... but you do need to understand cheeses, and choose and use them intelligently.

Basically, cheese is made from curdled milk. Since it takes approximately five quarts of milk to make one pound of cheese, it stands to reason that the concentration of fat and cholesterol in cheese would be high. The amount of fat and cholesterol varies, however, dependent upon the type of milk used (skim vs. lowfat vs. whole vs. cream).

Because of the increased consumer interest in lower fat foods, there have been many "modified" cheeses appear on the market in recent years. One can choose from cheeses which are low in fat, low in cholesterol, low in sodium, or a combination of all three. One low-cholesterol variety is referred to as filled cheese. Made from skim milk with vegetable oil added, filled cheese does contain fat. However, since vegetable oil contains no cholesterol, filled cheese contains considerably less cholesterol than regular varieties. The calorie value remains equal to regular cheese; the texture and melting characteristics are also similar. Occasionally, some regular cheese is added for flavor.

Low fat cheeses are widely available in supermarkets, and many are very good substitutes for higher fat cheeses in recipes. Be aware that some of these products, as well as all of the "no fat" cheeses, have different characteristics than real cheese when cooked or melted ... you cannot blanketly substitute them in all recipes. Read the labels and experiment on your own to determine which of these products you like and which work in your favorite recipes.

Generally speaking, if you are trying to maintain a low-fat and low-cholesterol diet, any cheese containing less than 1 gram of fat per ounce is made from skim milk and may be used without restriction. A cheese with 1-2 grams of fat per ounce is made primarily from skim milk, but due to higher fat should be used in moderation. A cheese with 3-5 grams of fat per ounce may be used in place of meat, probably not in addition to, as the saturated fat and cholesterol content is similar to one ounce of lean meat. With 6-8 grams of "low cholesterol" fat per ounce, filled skim milk cheeses may be eaten in addition to meat, unless one also needs to watch calorie intake. In this category, it is best to select products made with corn, safflower, or sunflower oils, avoiding varieties made with coconut or palm oils (which contain a great deal of saturated fat). Cheeses with 6-11 grams of fat per ounce are made from whole milk and contain a large amount of saturated fat and cholesterol. Use in small quantities and for special occasions is most appropriate for these varieties.

It is useful to remember that grating cheese for inclusion in or topping on a recipe is one way to use less and still get the wonderful flavor it provides.

These recipes for cheeses offer you homemade options for adding the flavor without the fat. They may be used to substitute for cream cheese, sour cream, and other whole milk soft cheeses. Many of the recipes in this book call for one of these alternative cheeses, and it is my hope that you'll develop recipes of your own using them.

HOMEMADE COTTAGE CHEESE

While excellent lowfat cottage cheeses are readily available in the supermarket, you may want to make your own with this simple recipe. Blenderized cottage cheese may be used in many recipes to substitute for higher fat cheeses and sour cream. A combination of cottage cheese and yogurt blended together (half of each) makes a nice base for numerous toppings, sauces, and recipes as a substitute for mayonnaise, sour cream, or heavy cream.

1 quart skim milk (or reconstituted nonfat dry milk)
3 tablespoons lemon juice (or cider vinegar)

Combine the ingredients and let stand 10 minutes to sour. Heat gently until soft curds form, about 15 minutes. Pour carefully into a cheese-cloth lined sieve or yogurt cheese funnel and let it drain completely. Break into small pieces with a fork. For creamier cottage cheese, moisten with a bit of nonfat yogurt.

Yield: 1/2 cup cottage cheese.

YOGURT CHEESE

High in protein and calcium, and low in fat, yogurt cheese is a multipurpose ingredient that can be used in many variations. When prepared this way, the yogurt is not as tart as yogurt and holds up well in cooking ... baking to a thick, firm texture like ricotta or cream cheese, blending as smoothly as sour cream into soups and sauces, and melting like butter on top of toast.

This process may be followed with any yogurt, plain or flavored, as long as it doesn't contain any gelatin or modified food starch which would hold the liquid whey in suspension so it can't drain off. The lower the fat in the yogurt, the better.

There are three possible devices you might use for making your yogurt cheese. The easiest is the "yogurt cheese funnel", a plastic mesh funnel made specifically for this purpose. You may also use a manual drip coffee filter or a strainer lined with a double layer of cheesecloth.

Set yogurt cheese funnel (or other device) on a stable jar large enough to hold liquid that drains off (you'll get about half as much liquid as there is yogurt; so, for example, for 2 cups of yogurt use at least a 1 cup container. Fill the funnel with yogurt. Cover top with plastic wrap. Place in refrigerator to drain. In several hours the yogurt will turn into a sour cream consistency. After 12-14 hours a soft cream cheese texture is achieved.

Yield: 1 cup yogurt cheese for every 2 cups of yogurt.

BREAKFAST CHEESE

Another alternative soft cheese delicious in spreads and recipes, this breakfast cheese is easy to make. It can be kept refrigerated for about 2 weeks.

1 quart skim milk
1/2 cup lowfat cultured buttermilk

Mix milk and buttermilk together in a stainless steel or glass bowl and choose a larger pot that will contain it. Cover the bowl with plastic wrap and let stand at room temperature at least one full day. Fill the large pot with very hot tap water and place the bowl with the milk mixture inside. After 2-3 minutes, water will begin to appear around the edges of the mixture. Turn the heat on, start timing, and heat for 5 minutes, keeping the water just below a boil. A white, curdy mass will form. Remove the pot from the water bath, put it on a rack and cool for 1-2 hours.

Ladle the contents of the pot into cheesecloth or a fine strainer set over a bowl. Drain for at least 2 hours. Put the cheese in a jar, cover and refrigerate.

Yield: 1 1/2 cups cheese.

SOUR MINUS CREAM

Another low fat substitute for sour cream comes from "Jane Brody's Nutrition Book". This book is a scholarly but practical guide to basic nutrition written by the well known personal health columnist for The New York Times. She offers scientifically-based information on various aspects of human nutrition, as well as specific tips for feeding people at all stages of life. I highly recommend her book to anyone looking for a reliable source for nutrition information. (see Reading List on page 159)

1 cup lowfat creamed cottage cheese
2 tablespoons skim milk
1 tablespoon lemon juice (or vinegar)
1/4 teaspoon salt

Put all ingredients in a blender container and blend at medium high speed until smooth and creamy. May be served cold or added to hot dishes at the last moment.
Yield: 1 cup.

SPICED CHEESE

This variation of cheese makes a nice addition to breakfast - served with whole grain bread, or as a filling for whole wheat crepes topped with a medley of lightly cooked vegetables. As an appetizer, Spiced Cheese may be used as a dip for vegetables. It may also be thinned a bit and used as a salad dressing.

1 cup lowfat cottage cheese
3 tablespoons nonfat yogurt
1 tablespoon chopped scallions or chives
1 tablespoon fresh parsley
1/4 teaspoon dried thyme
Freshly ground black pepper

Place all ingredients in a blender. Blend thoroughly until smooth and creamy. Keeps well in refrigerator for at least a week.
Yield: 1 1/4 cups.

OLD WORLD STYLE BAKED CHEESES

Pot-style cheese is as old as human civilization itself. These delicious baked cheeses simulate some of the exotic cheeses flavored with vegetables, fruit, nuts, and herbs found in traditional cultures. Ingredients are different for these two recipes, but the method is the same.

Vegetable Baked Cheese

1 cup yogurt cheese
1 stalk celery, finely chopped
2 scallions, finely chopped
1 small carrot, shredded
1 teaspoon dill seed
1/2 teaspoon salt

Fruit Baked Cheese

1 cup yogurt cheese
1/4 cup chopped raisins, dried
    apricots, and/or pitted dried cherries
1 tablespoon honey
2 tablespoons orange juice
1/2 teaspoon minced orange rind

Preheat oven to 350°. Combine all ingredients and place in a 10-ounce ramekin. Bake 30 minutes. Cool to room temperature, pour off any accumulated liquid, unmold, and chill completely before serving.

Yield: 1 cheese round.

COEUR A LA CREME

Usually a very rich, high fat dessert, this "coeur" (heart) is "coeur-healthy". This recipe calls for a 4-cup heart shaped mold for the cheese, but we use little individual heart shaped molds for a more personal presentation.

3 ounces Neufchatel cheese, softened
1 container (16-ounce) lowfat cottage cheese
1 container (15-ounce) part-skim ricotta cheese
1 container (16-ounce) nonfat plain yogurt
1/2 cup sugar
1 tablespoon grated orange rind
1 teaspoon vanilla
Strawberry sauce (recipe follows)

Beat together Neufchatel, cottage, and ricotta cheeses. With mixer on low speed, beat in yogurt until blended. Line large sieve with double layer of cheesecloth. Place over a large bowl. Scrape cheese mixture into lined sieve. Fold ends of cheesecloth over, cover with plastic wrap. Fit a plate over the cheese mixture and top with a 1-pound can to weigh down. Refrigerate overnight, discarding drained liquid.

Turn drained mixture into large bowl. Stir in sugar, orange rind, and vanilla. Line 4-cup heart mold with plastic wrap. Top with double layer of cheesecloth. Fill with mixture. Fold ends of cheesecloth and plastic wrap over mixture. Refrigerate for at least 4 hours.

To serve, unwrap ends of cheesecloth and plastic wrap. Invert serving platter over mold. Carefully turn over. Remove mold, plastic wrap and cheesecloth. Surround with Strawberry Sauce and garnish with fresh strawberries.

Yield: 12 servings.

Strawberry Sauce

Combine 1 package (10-ounce) frozen strawberries, thawed, and 1/4 teaspoon almond extract in blender or food processor. Process until smooth. Makes 1 cup.

(Note: Juice from strawberries can cause the Coeur a la Creme to separate and crack, so berries are served on the side, not on top.)

BON APPETITE!